Colour Me Diva

for

Quick Break Colouring In

Get the pencils, inks and even

make-up ready to add your own

individual style

Relax, feet up and enjoy.

ISBN:1542445442
ISBN-13:9781542445443

FOR MY GOOD FRIEND DEBBIE

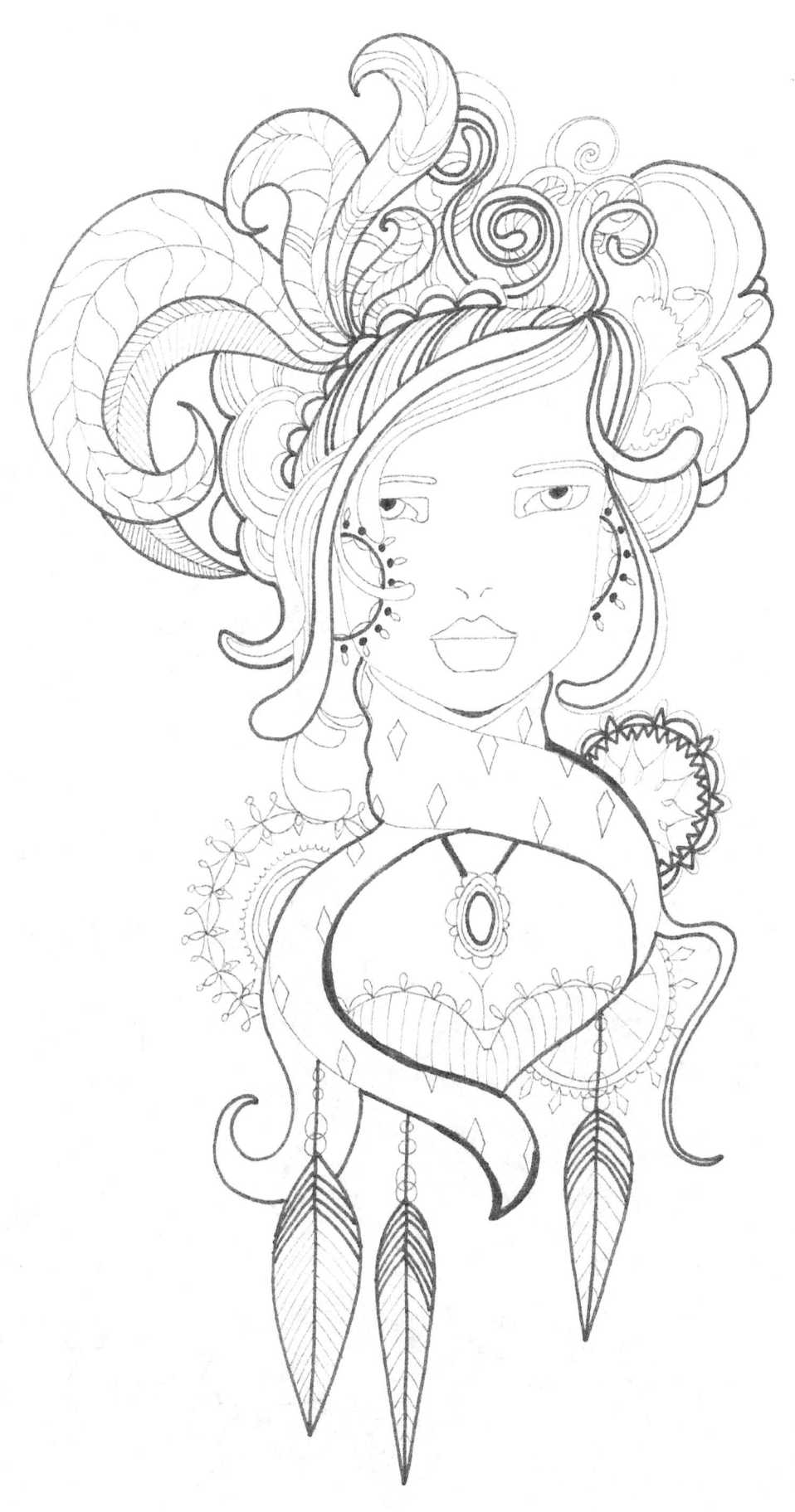

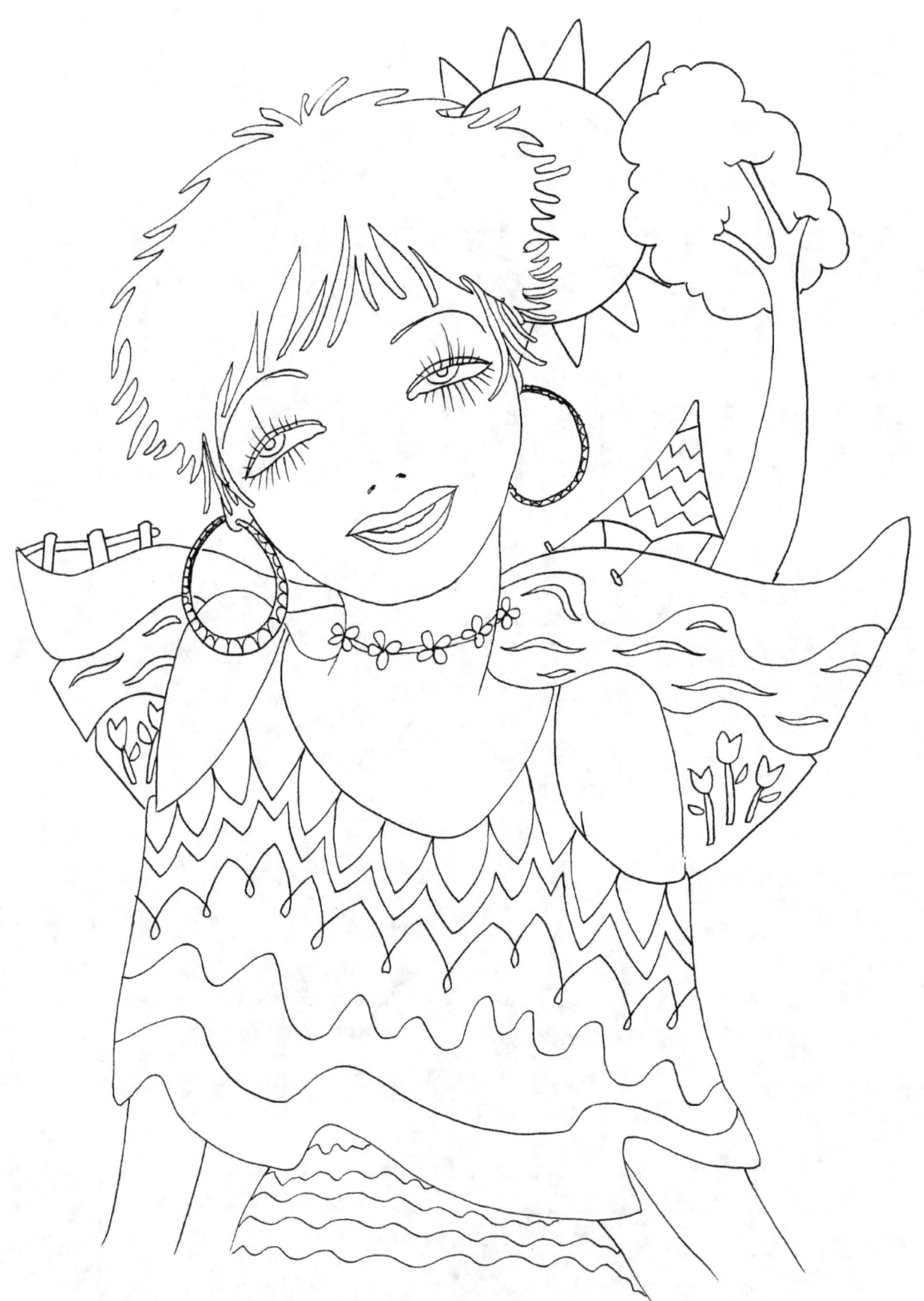

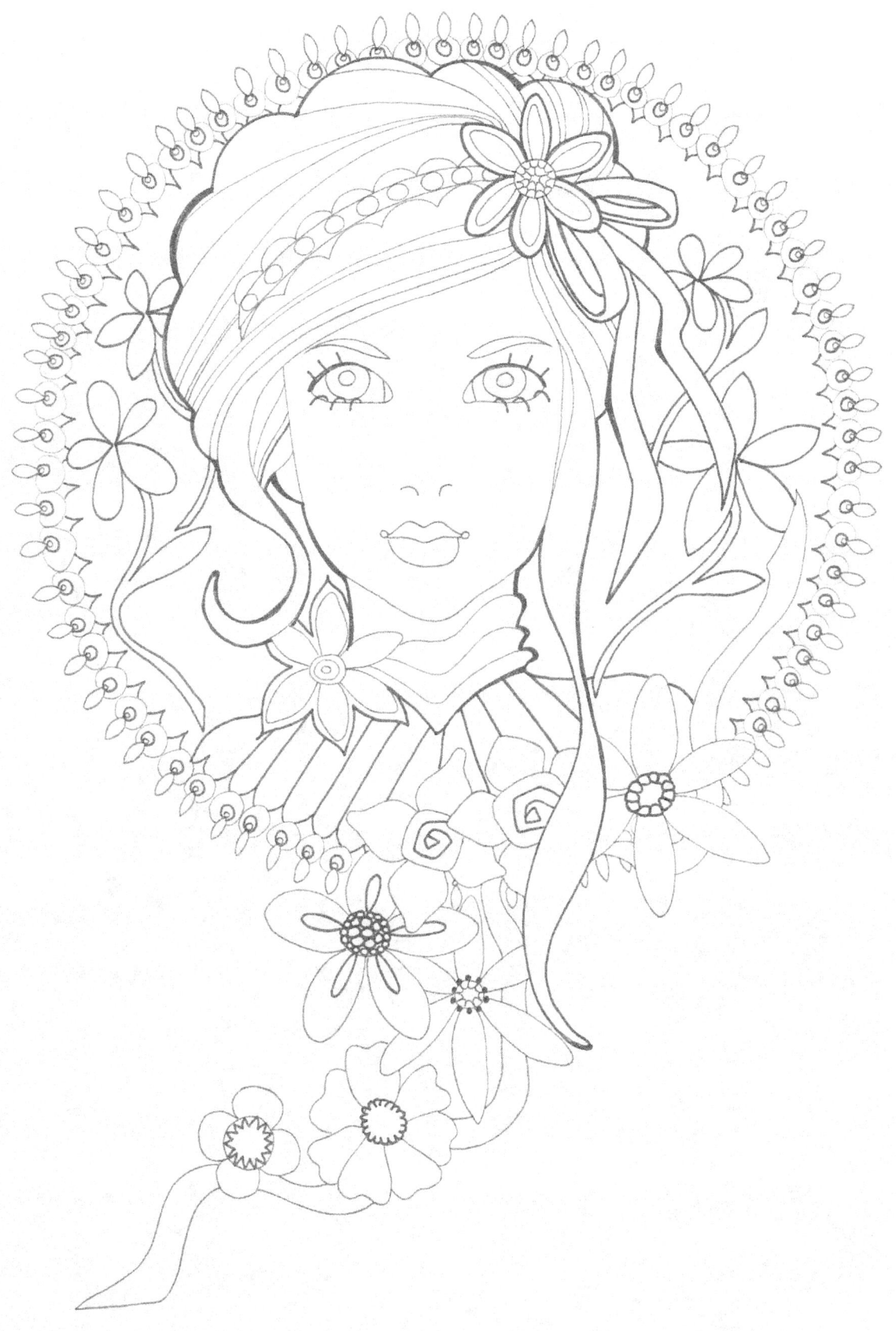

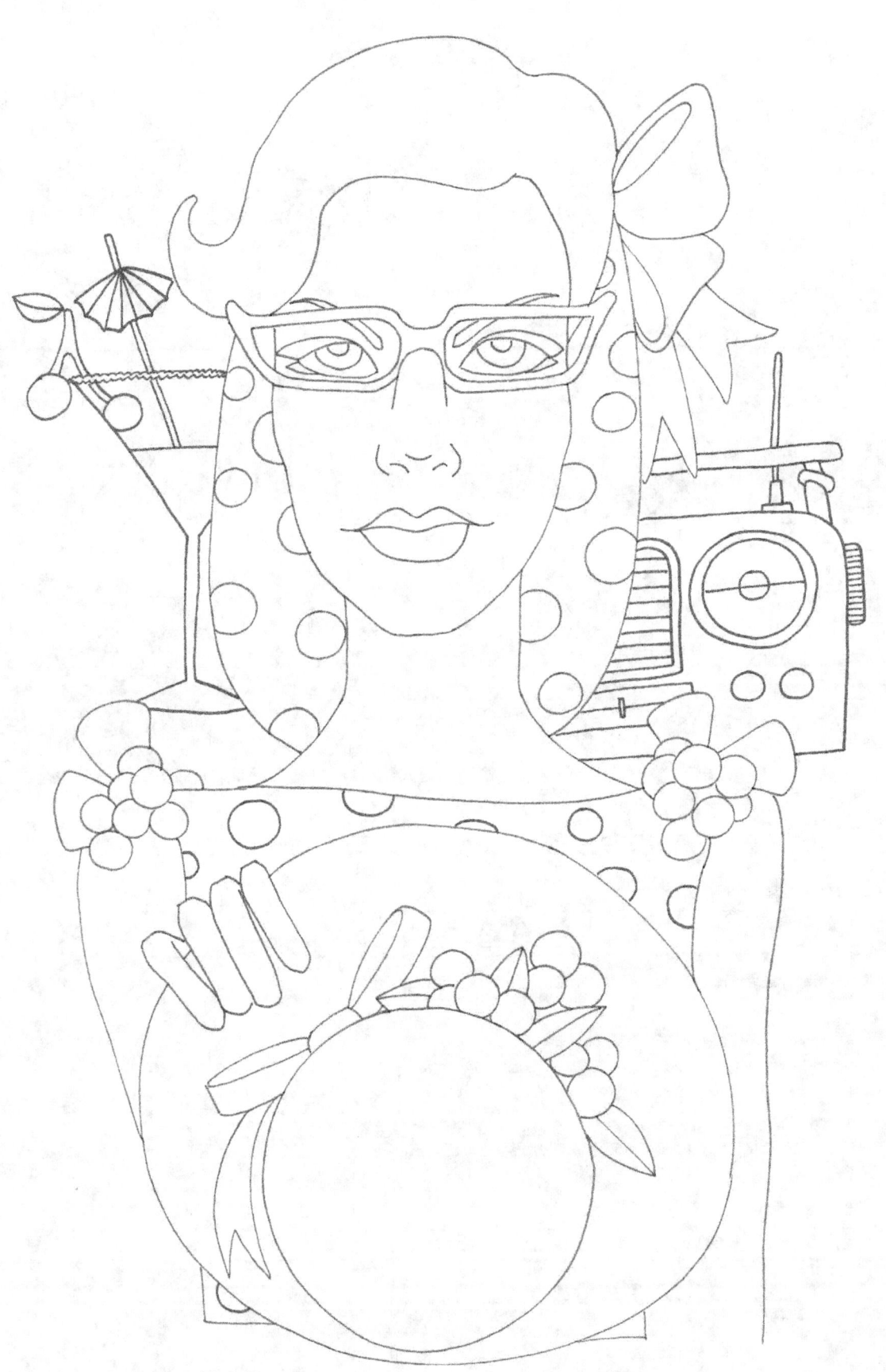

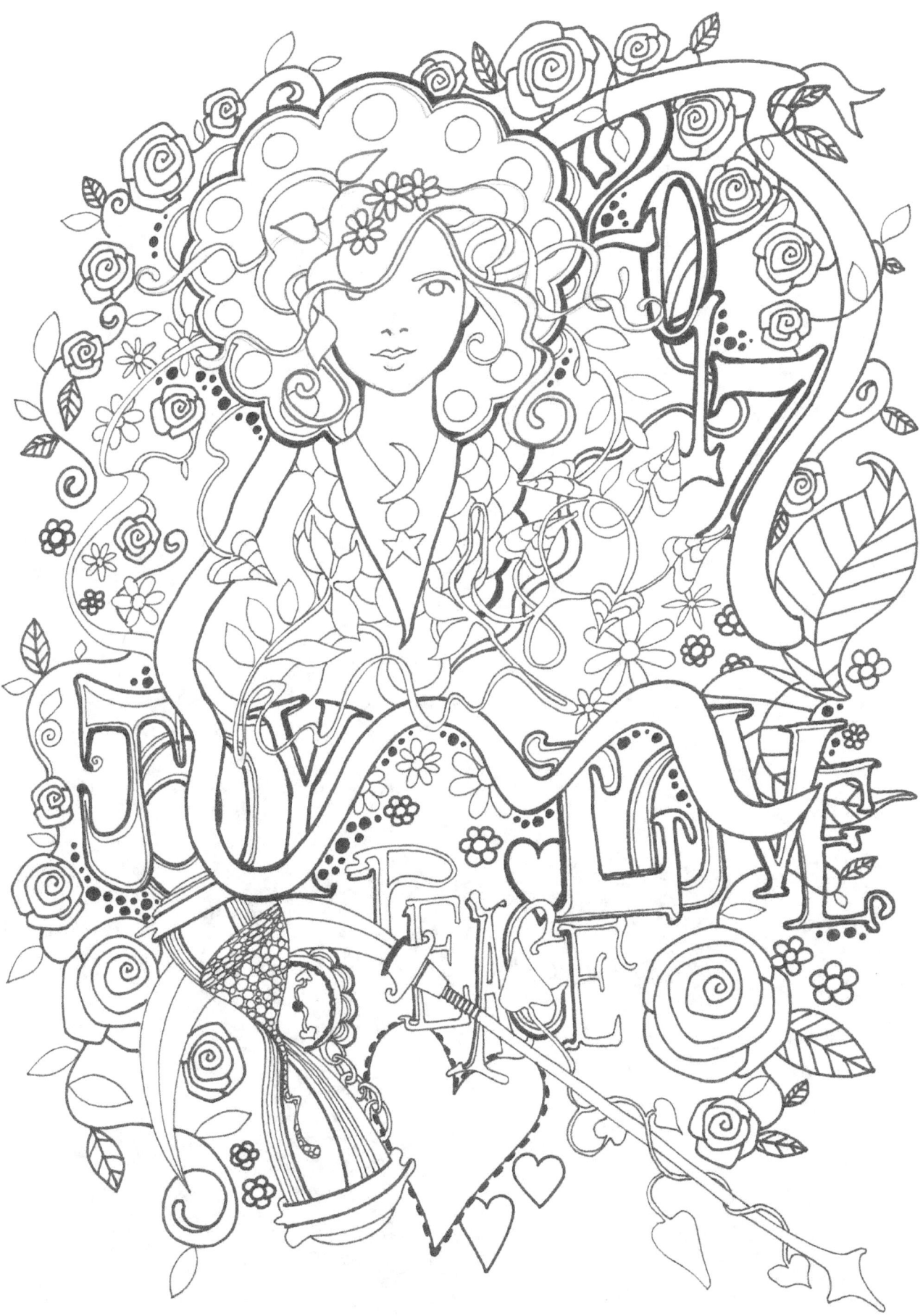

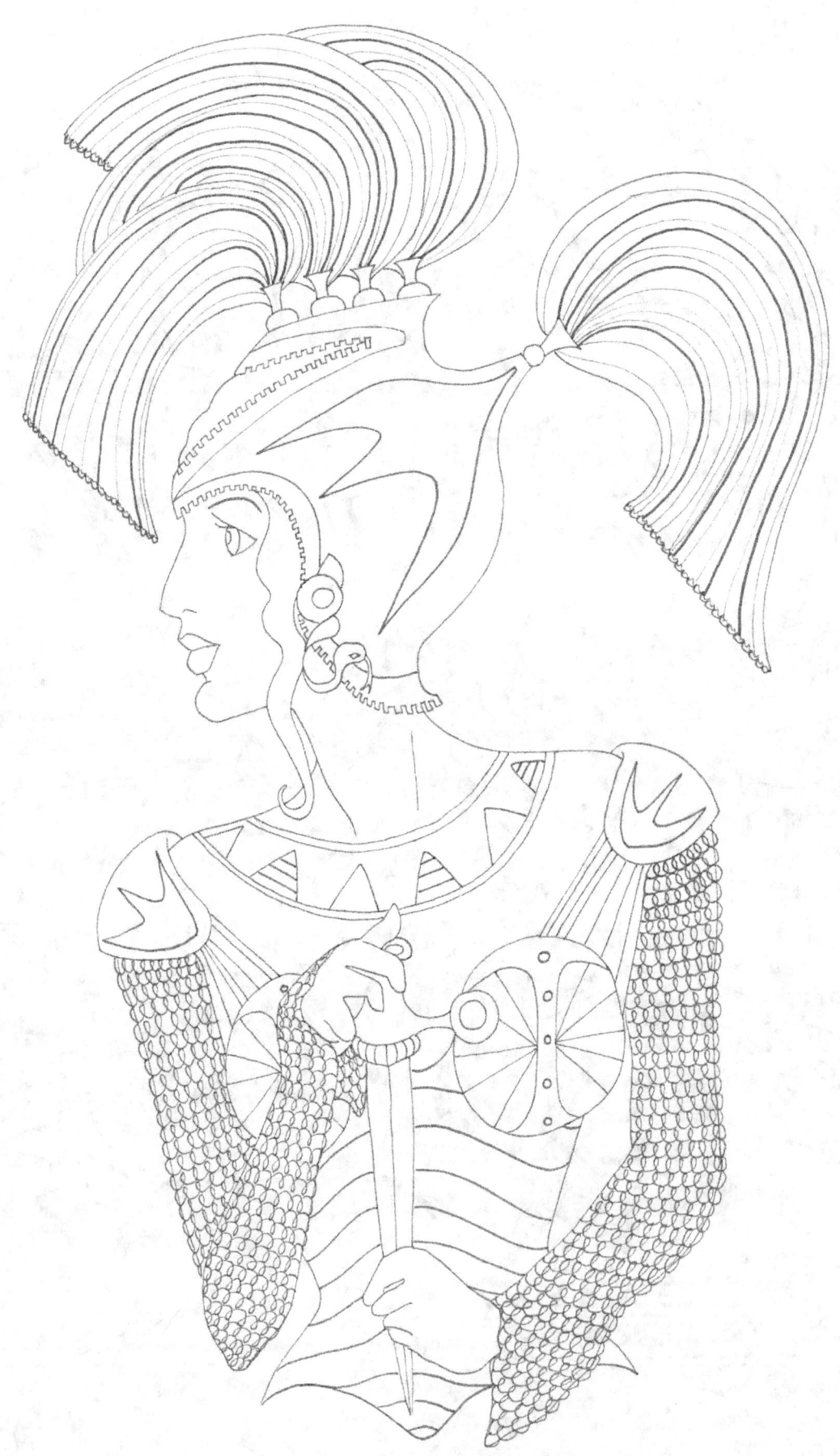

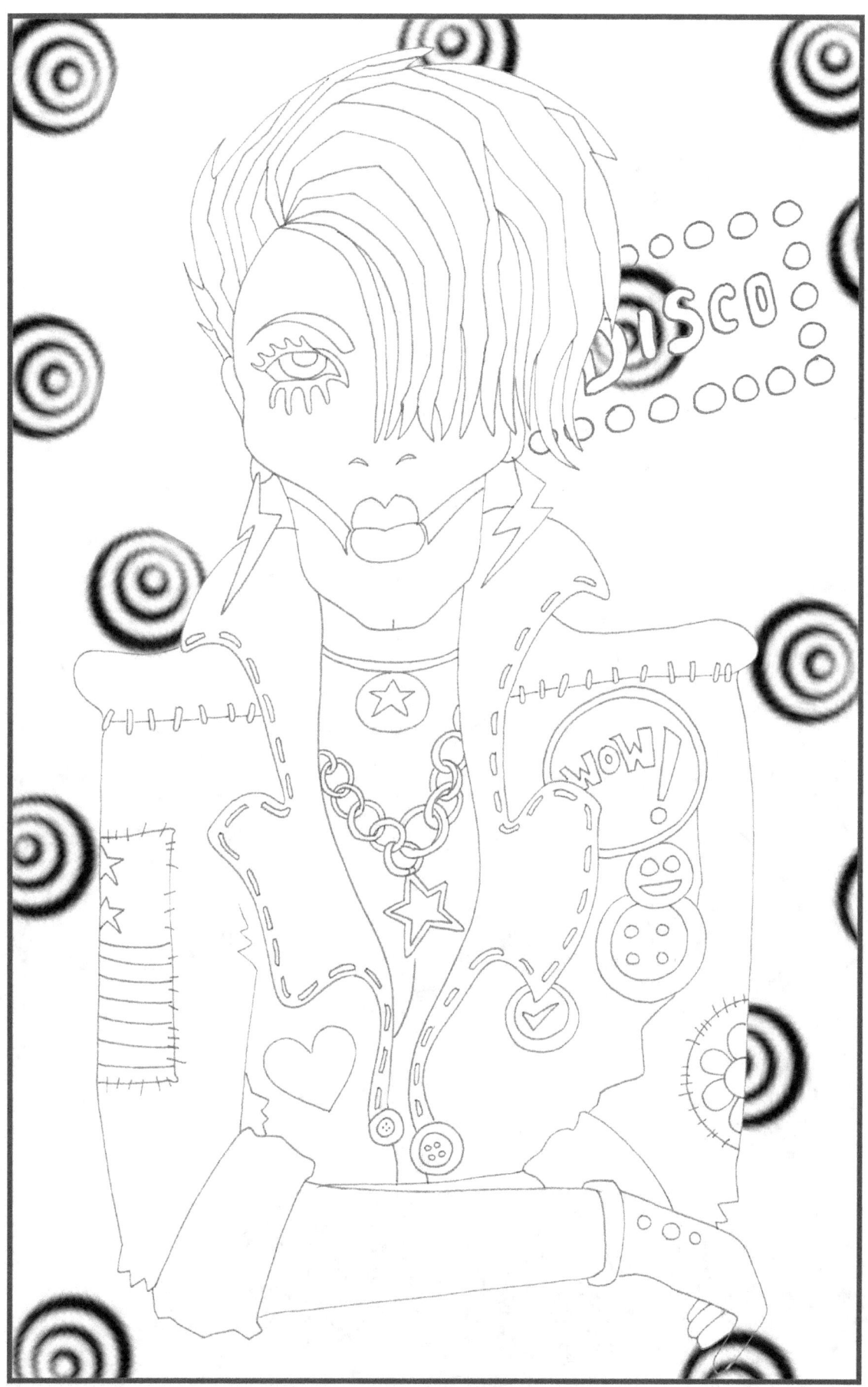

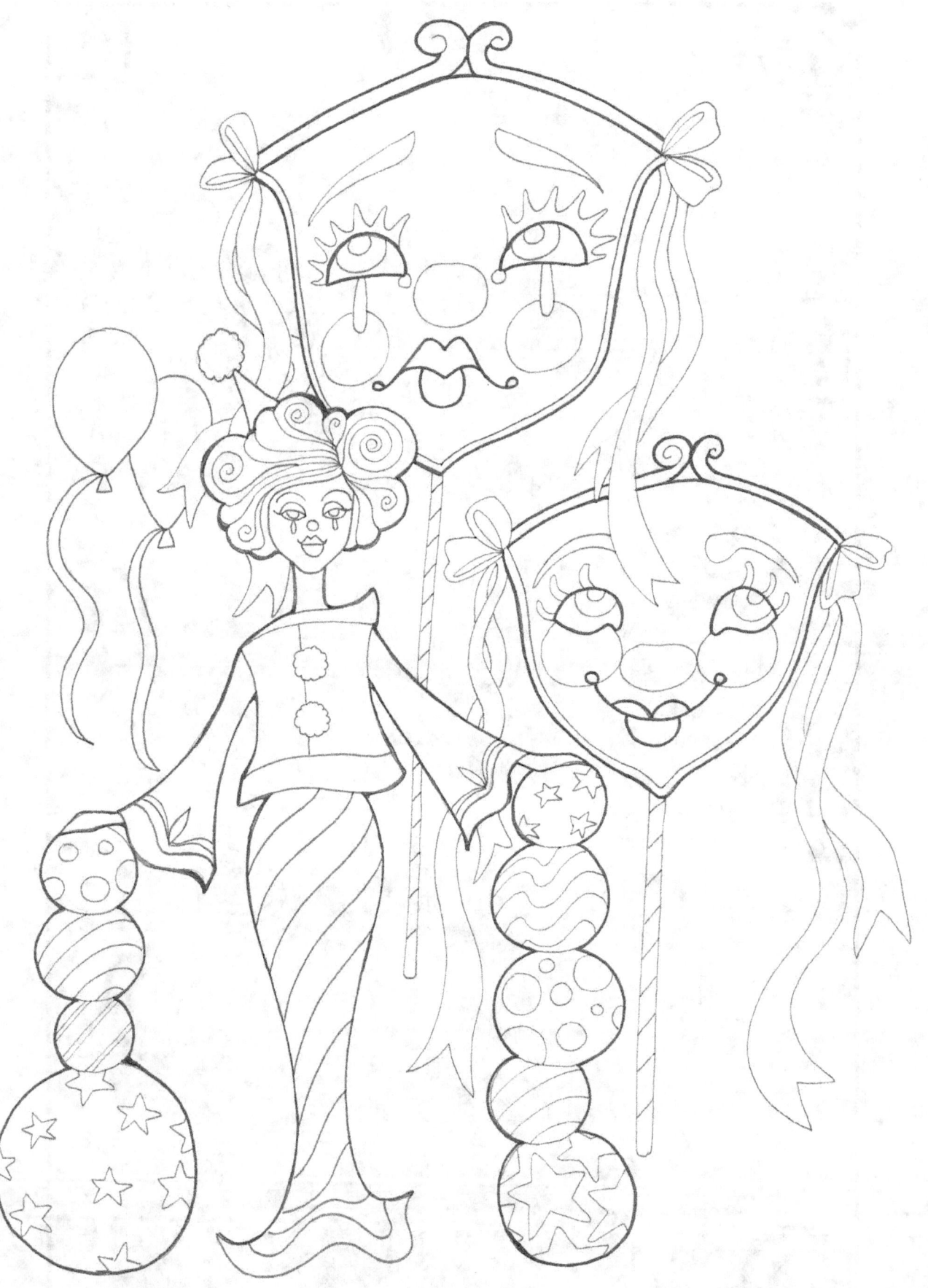

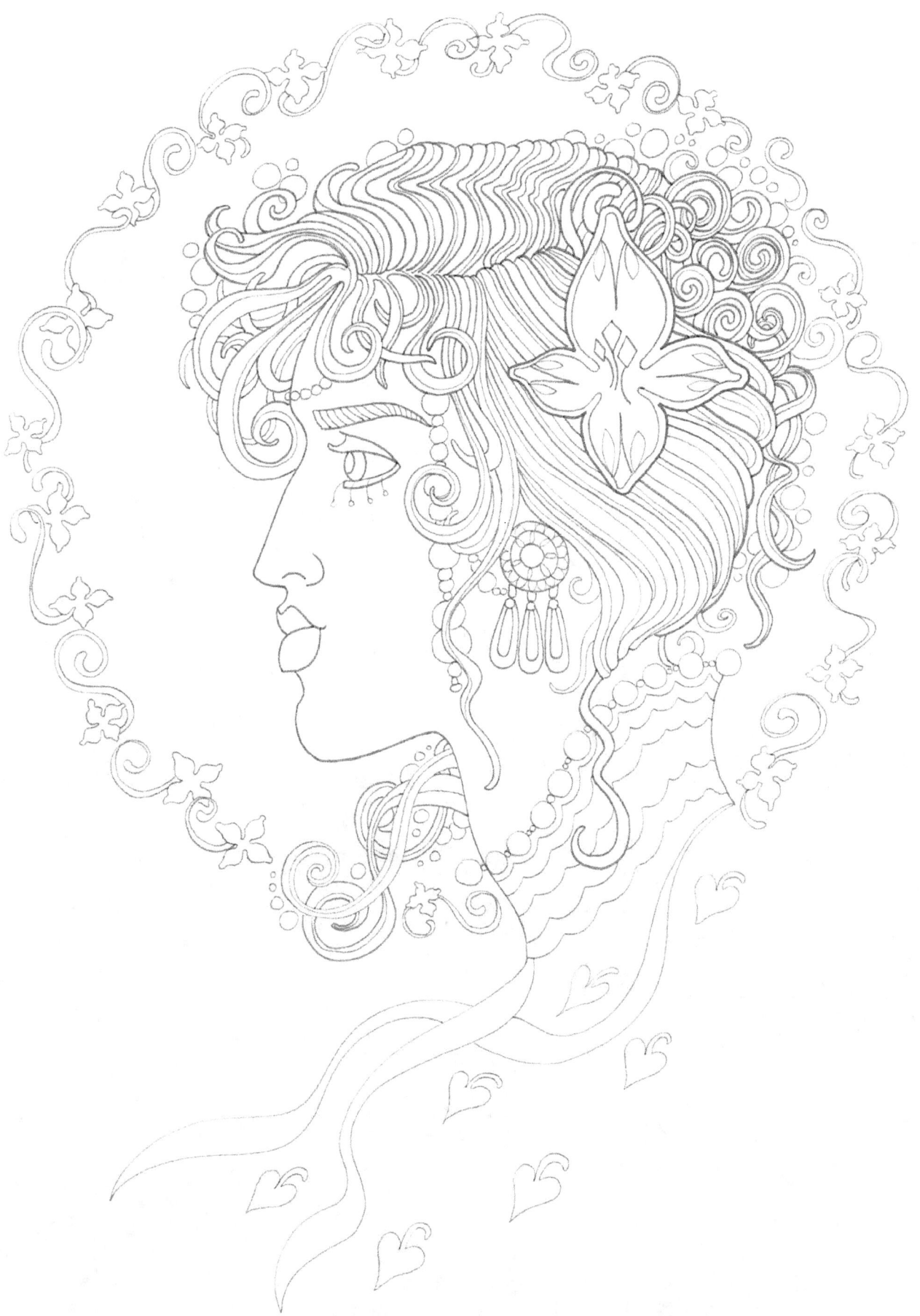

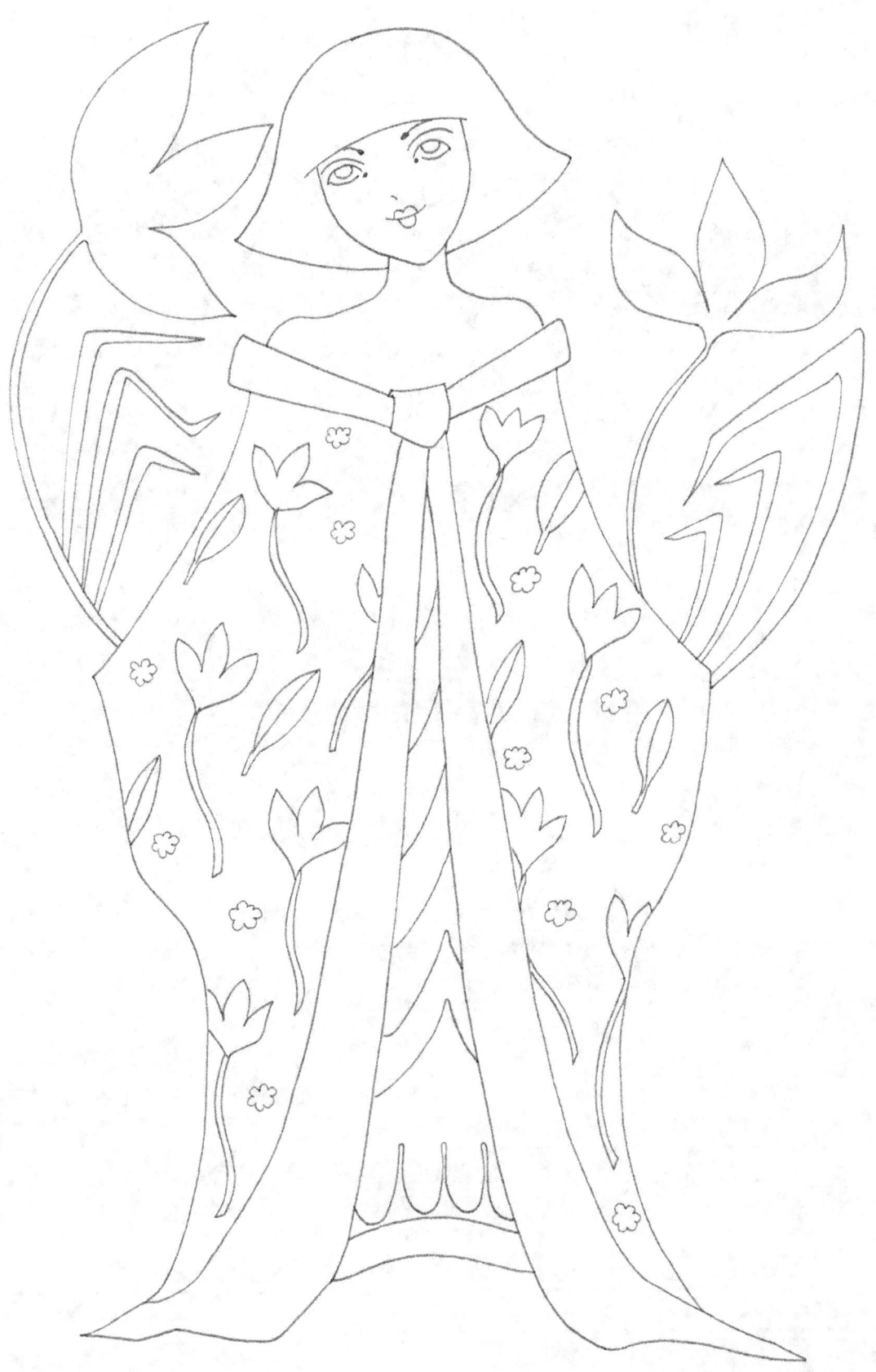

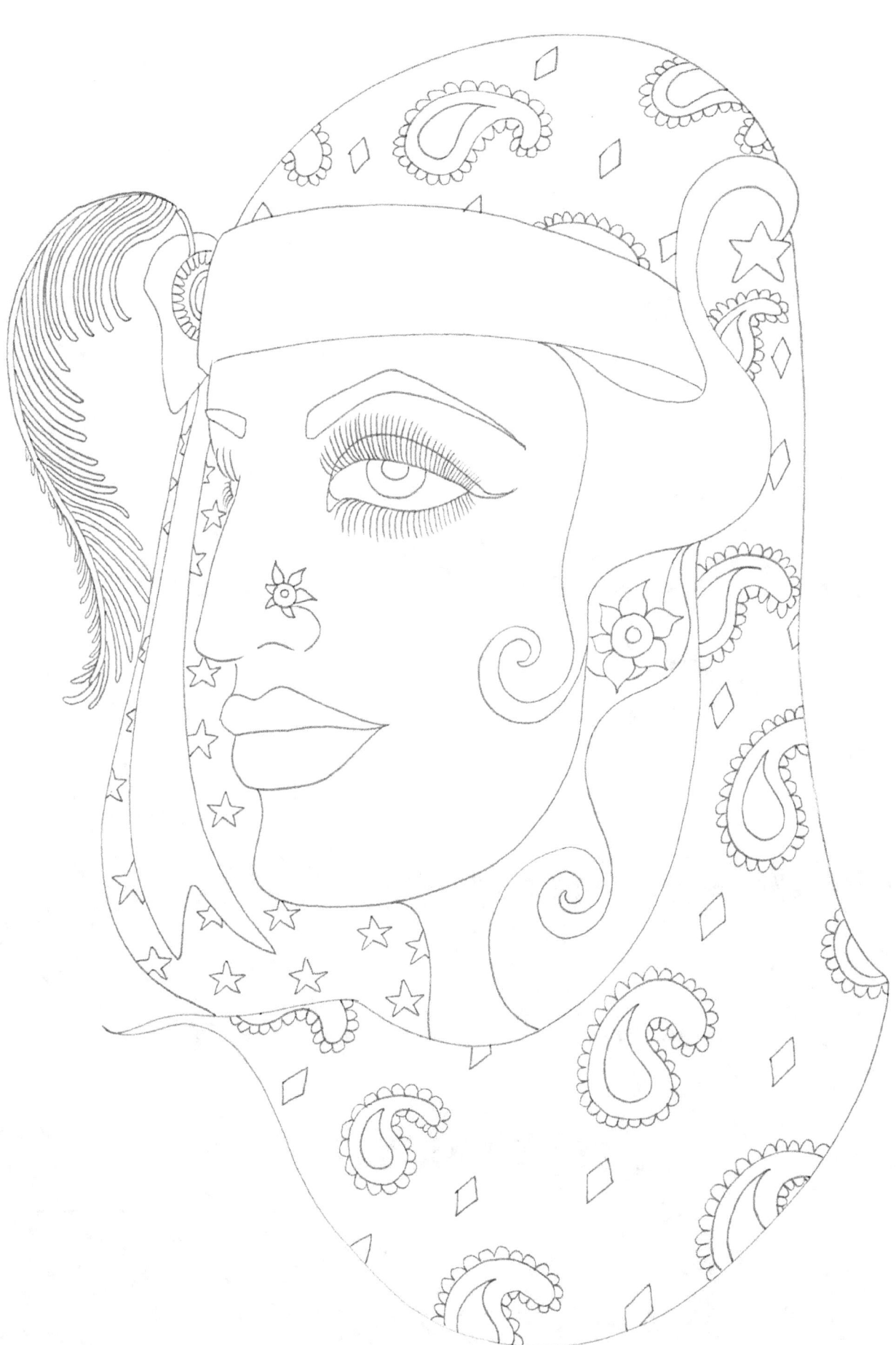

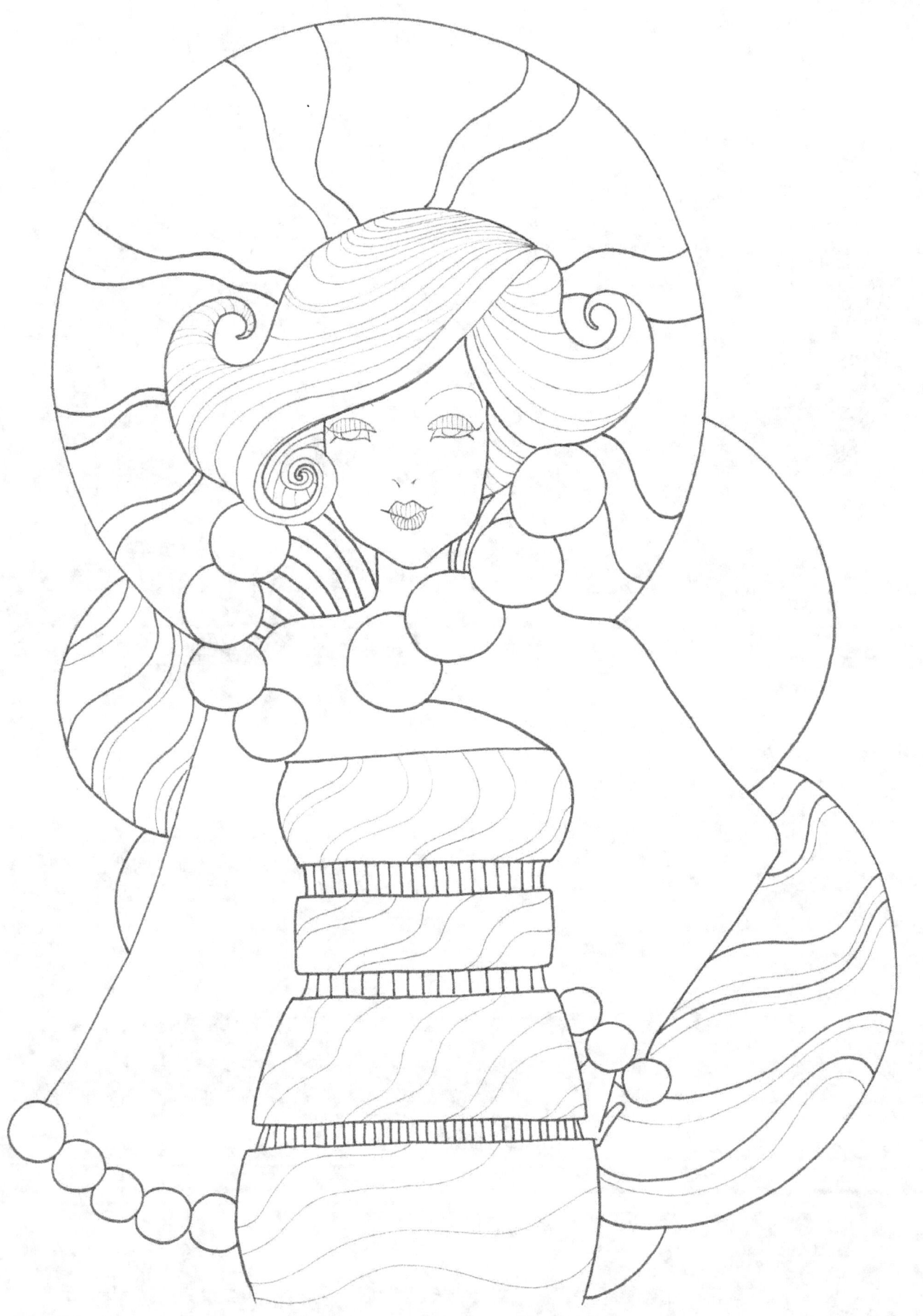

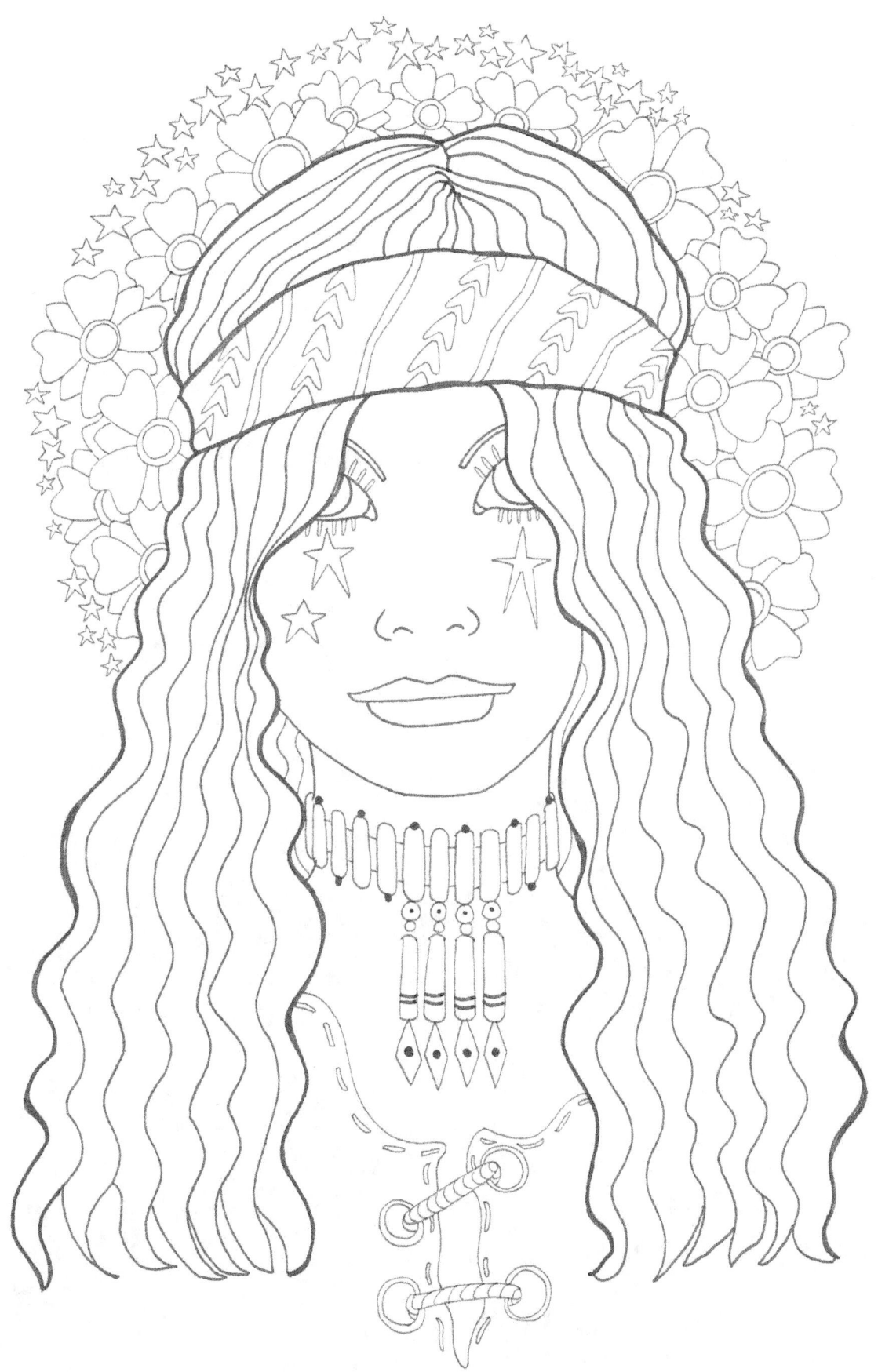

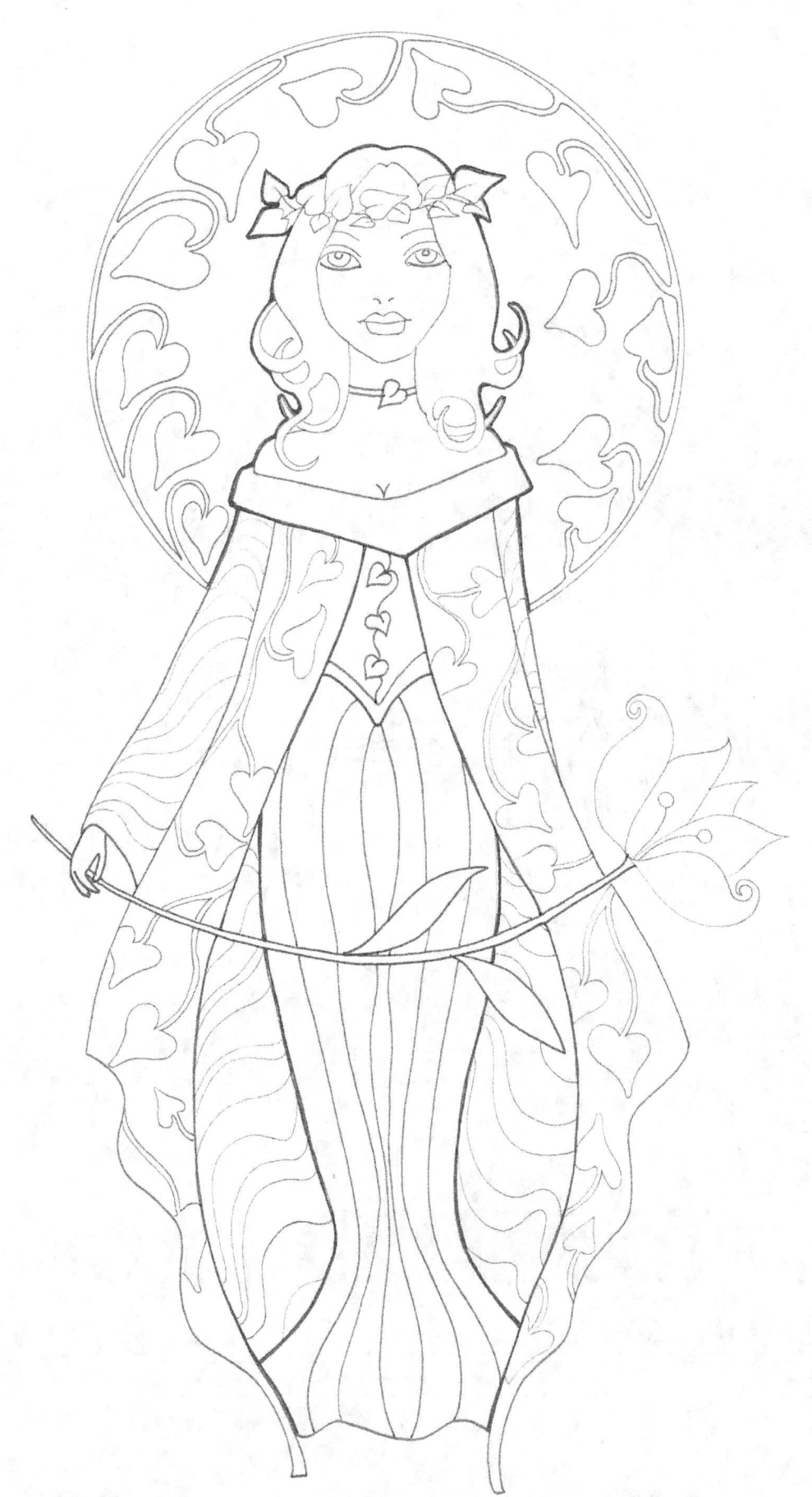

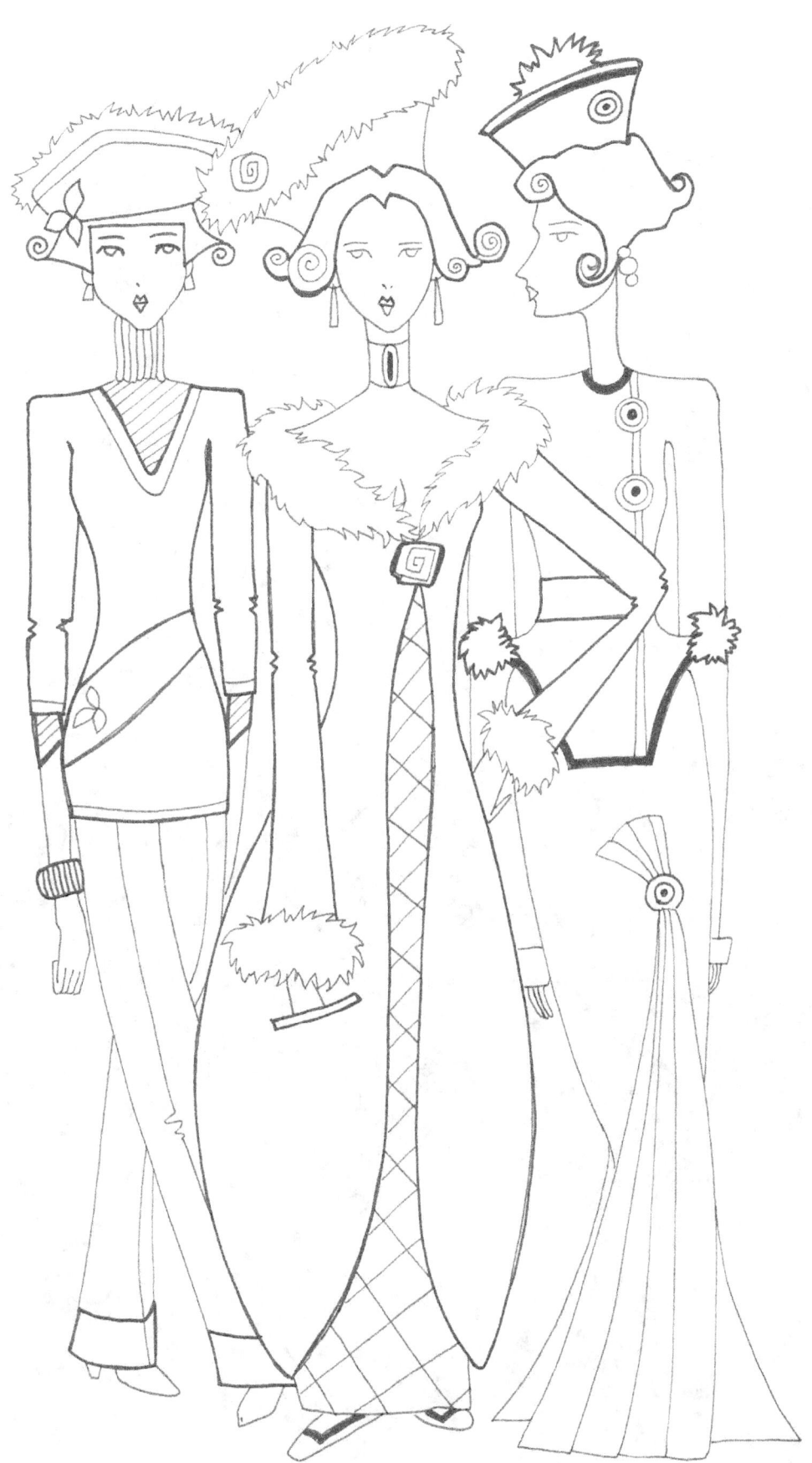

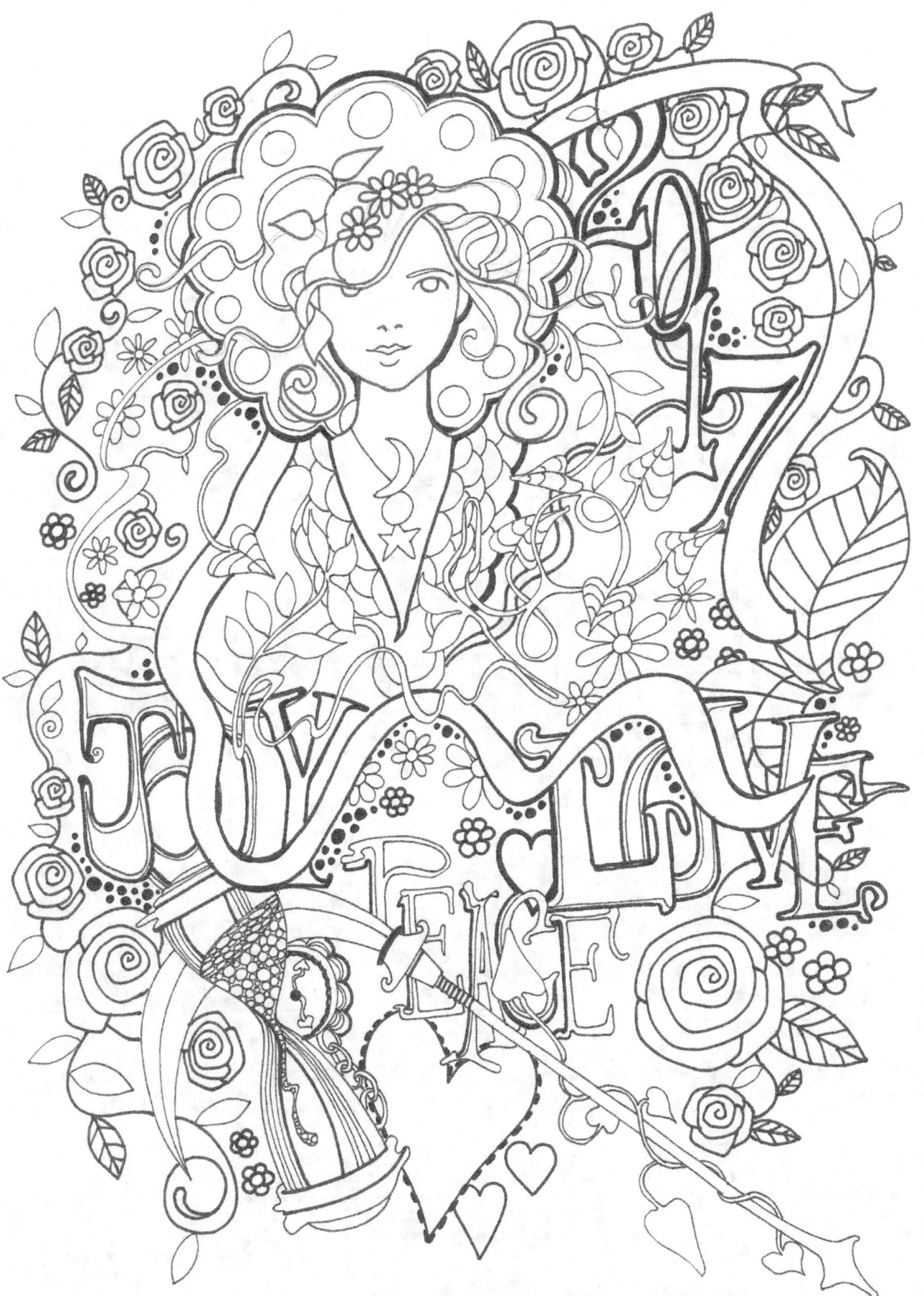

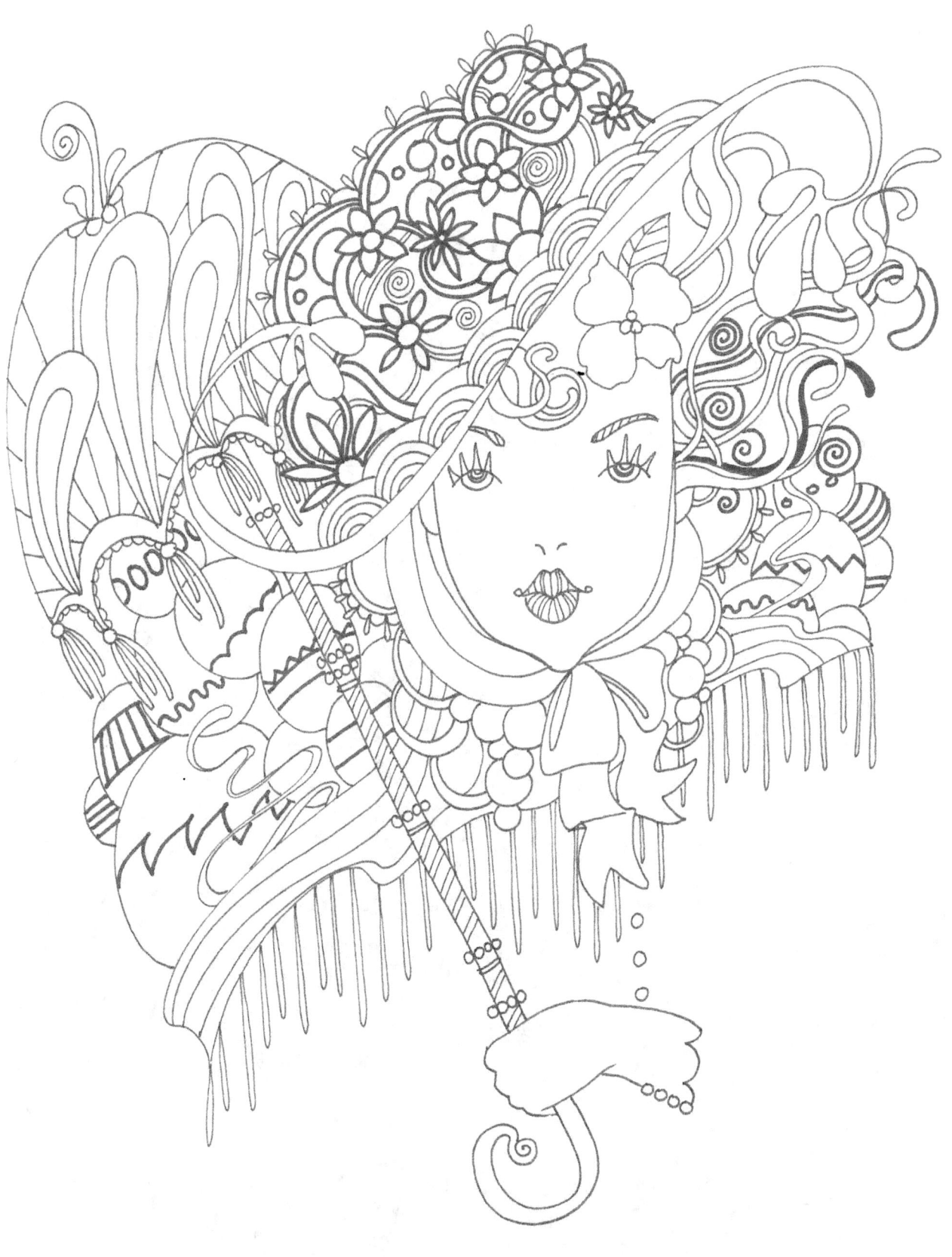

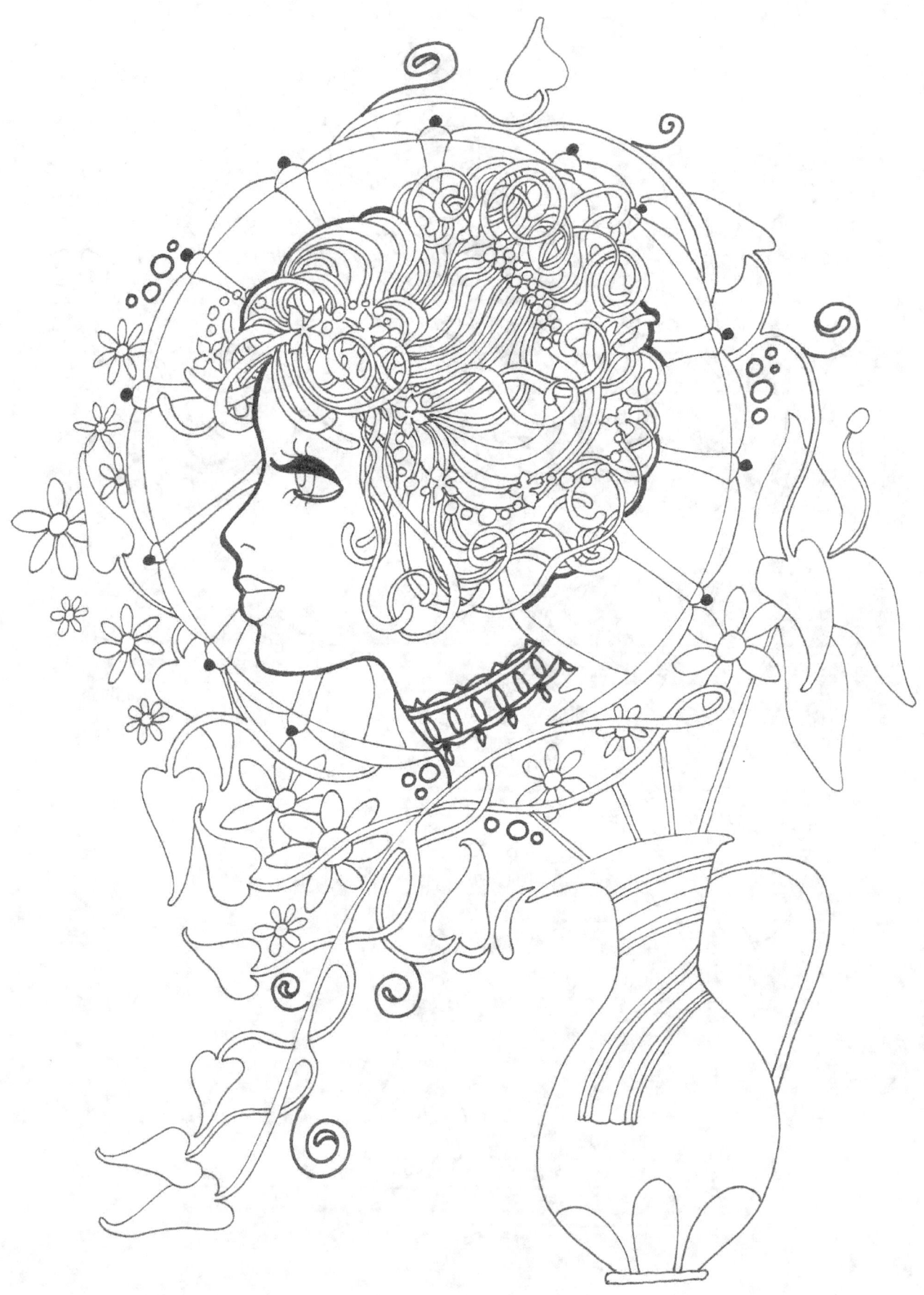

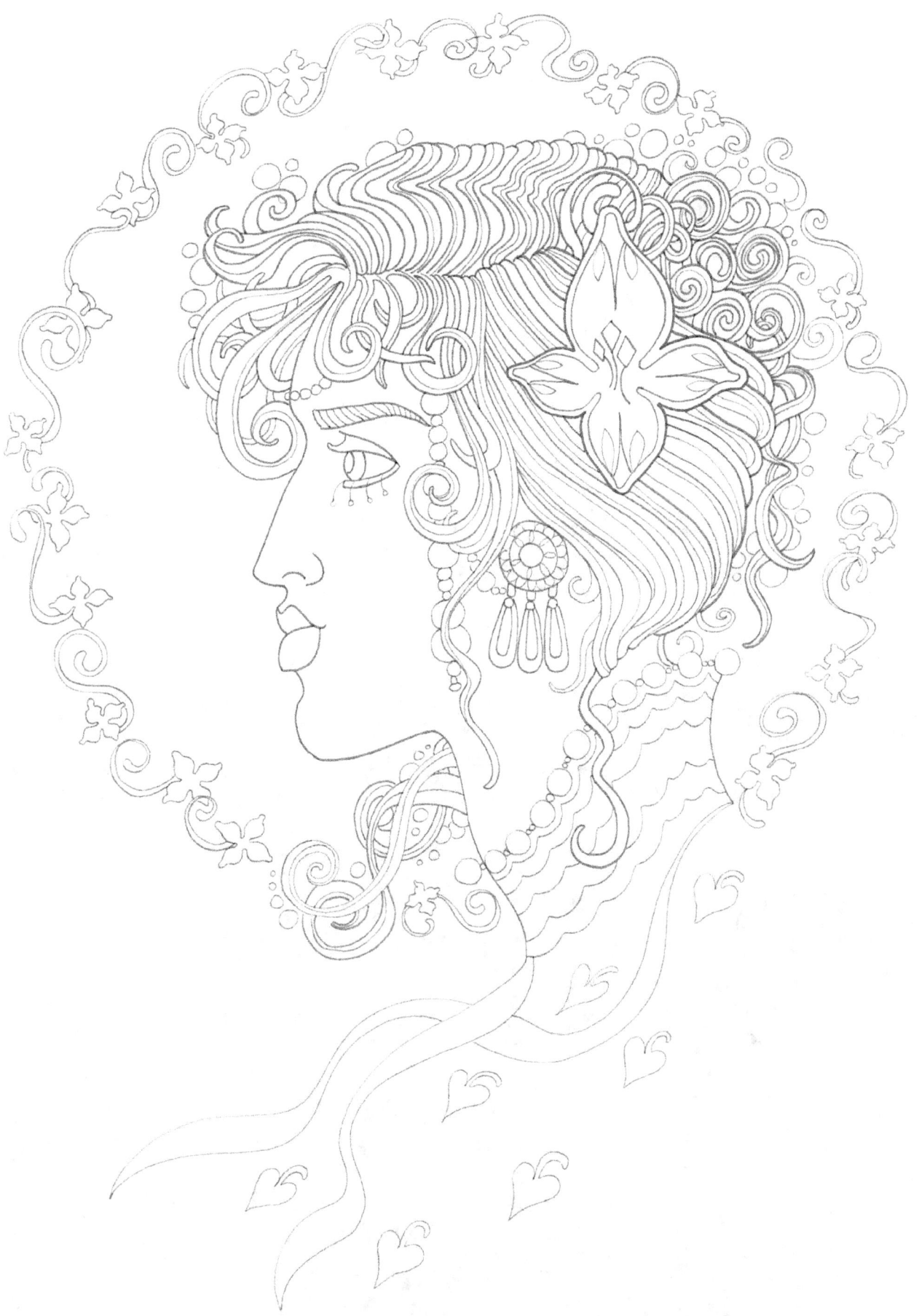

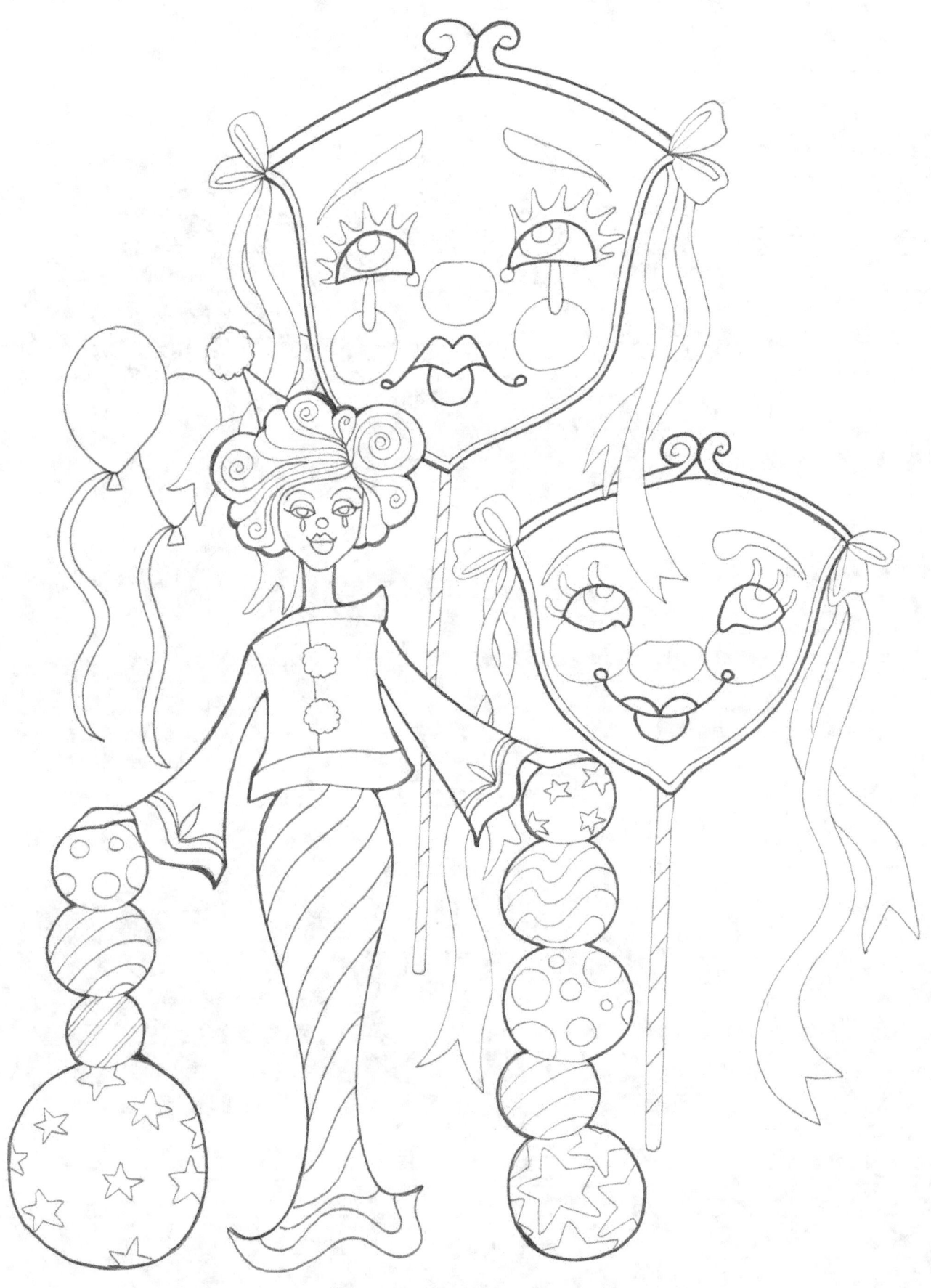

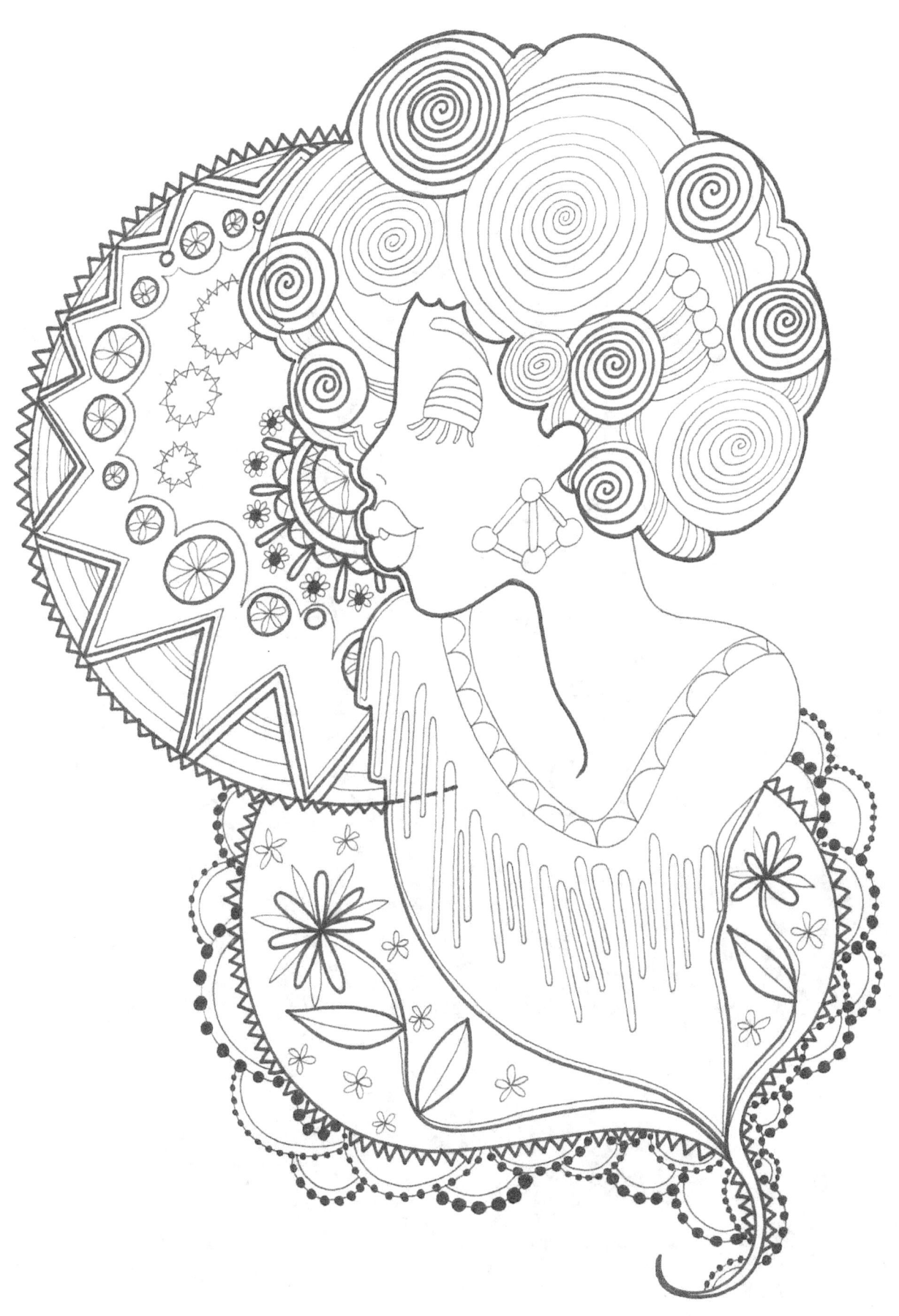

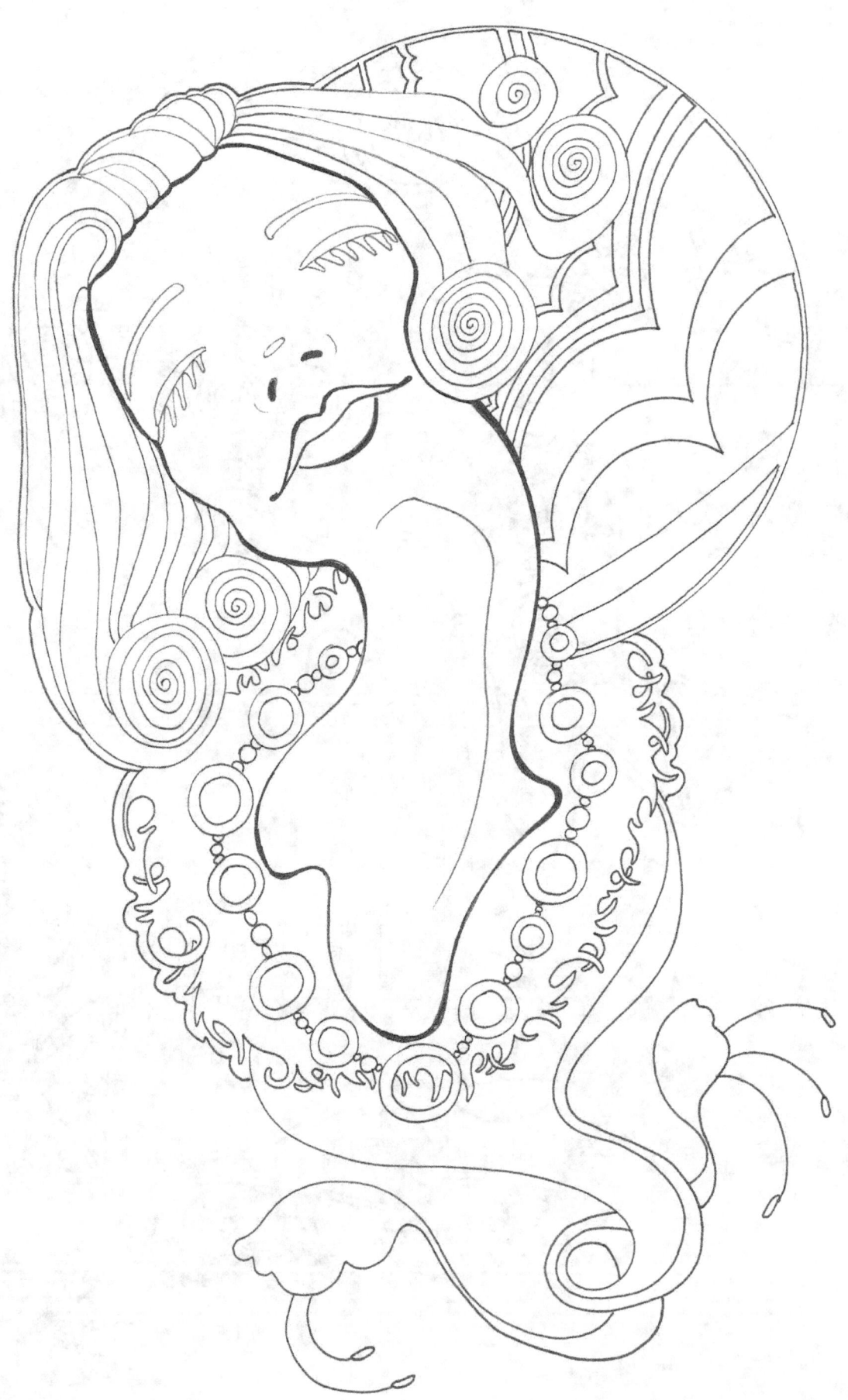

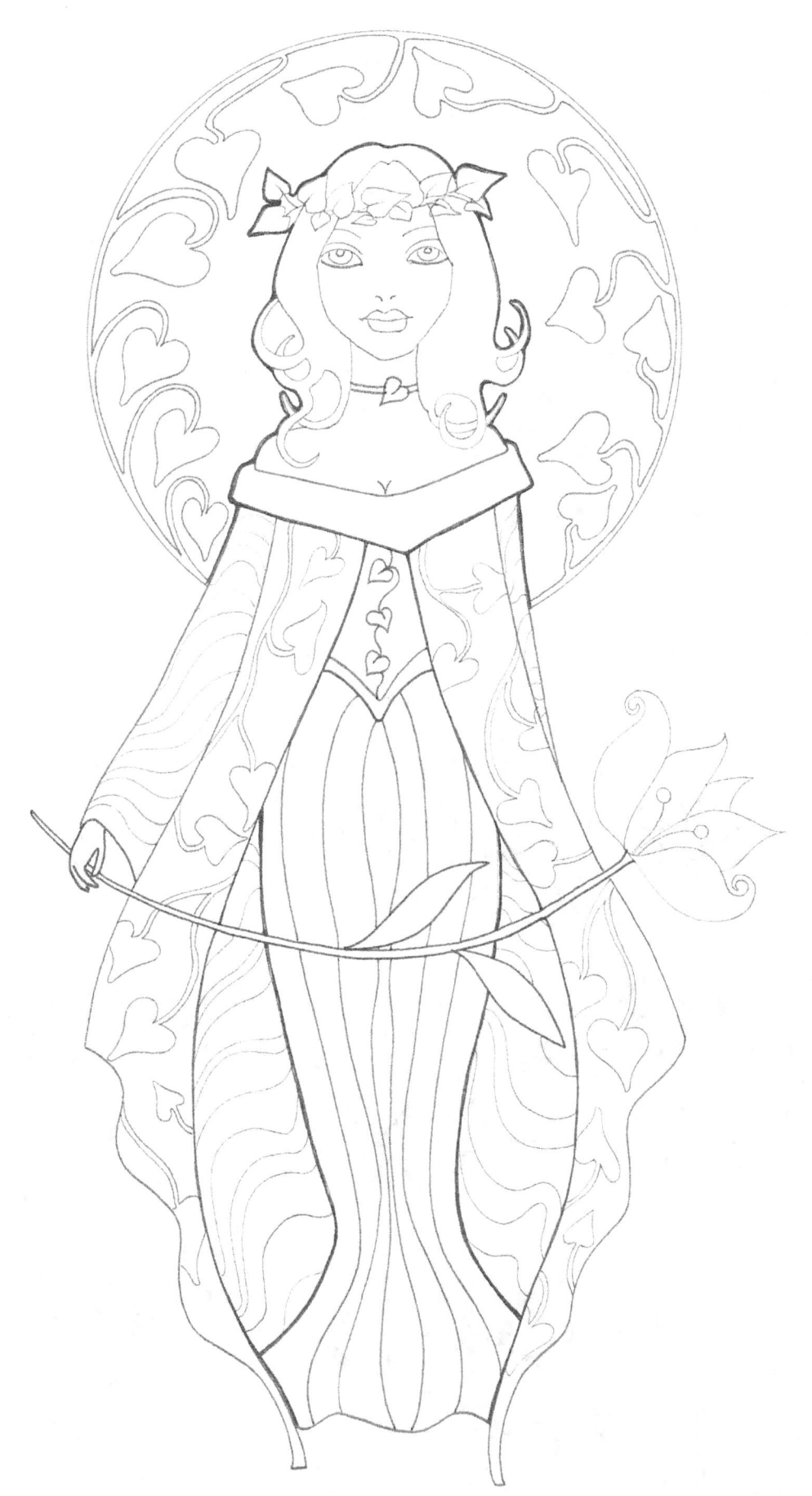

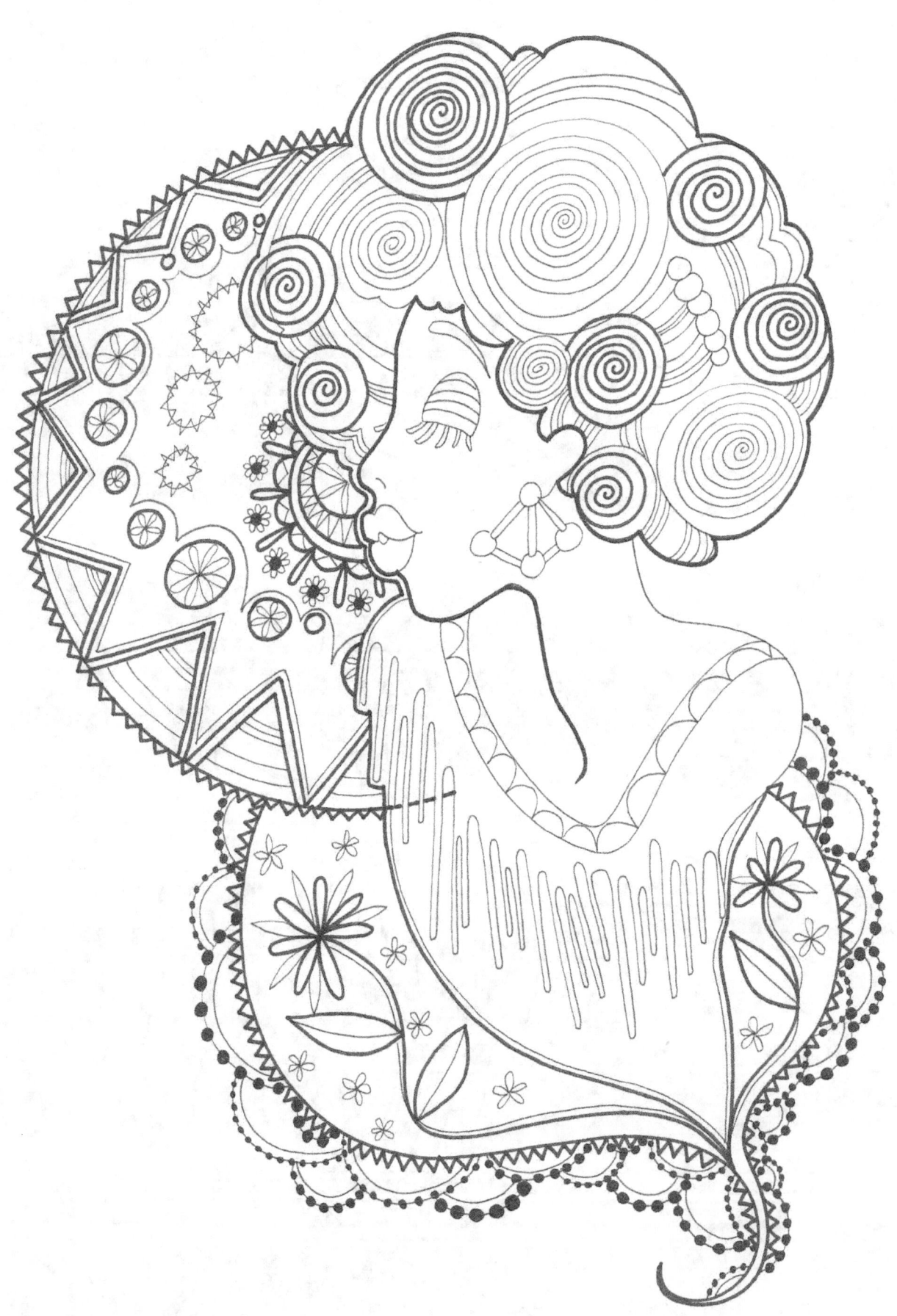

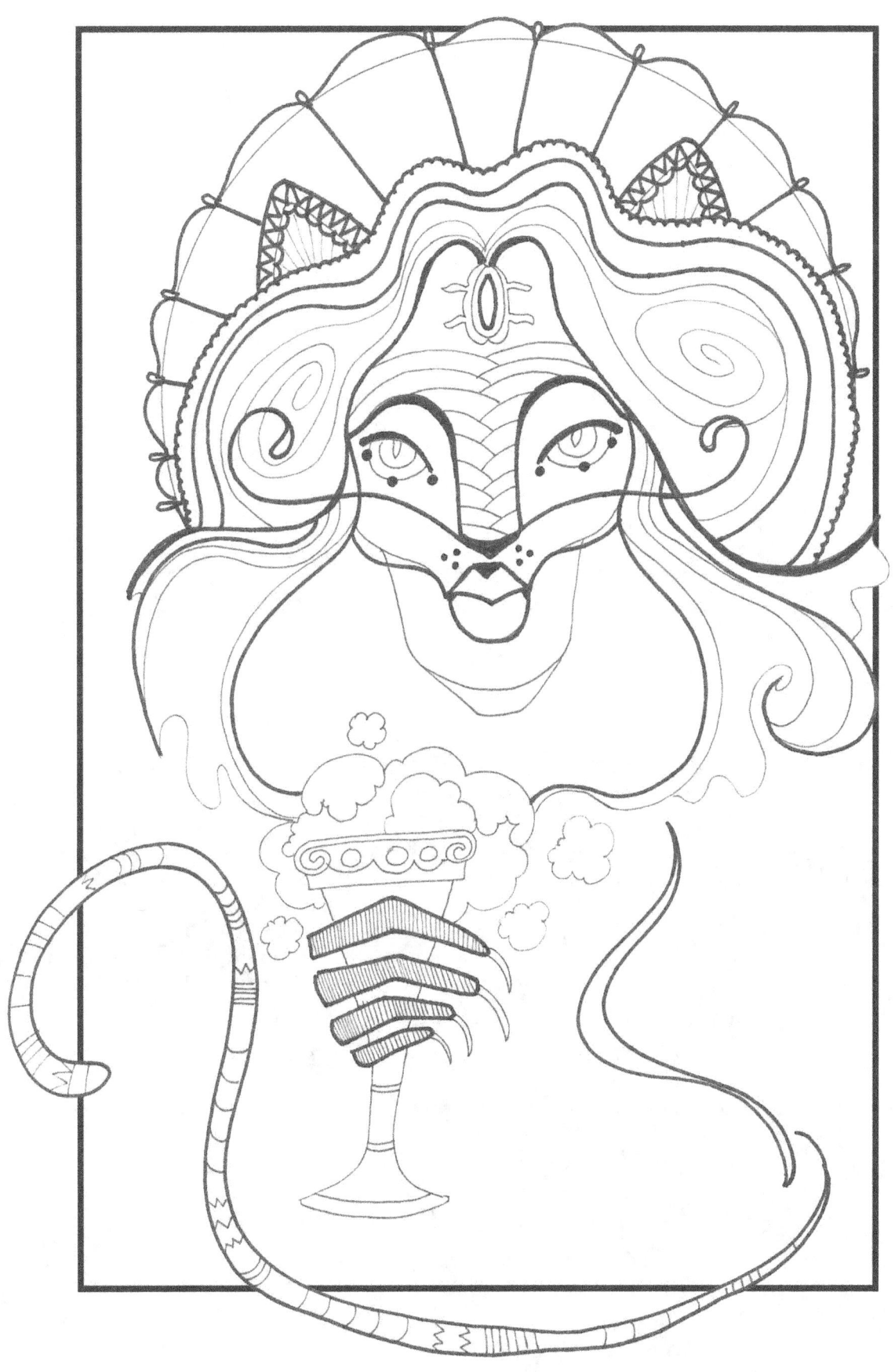

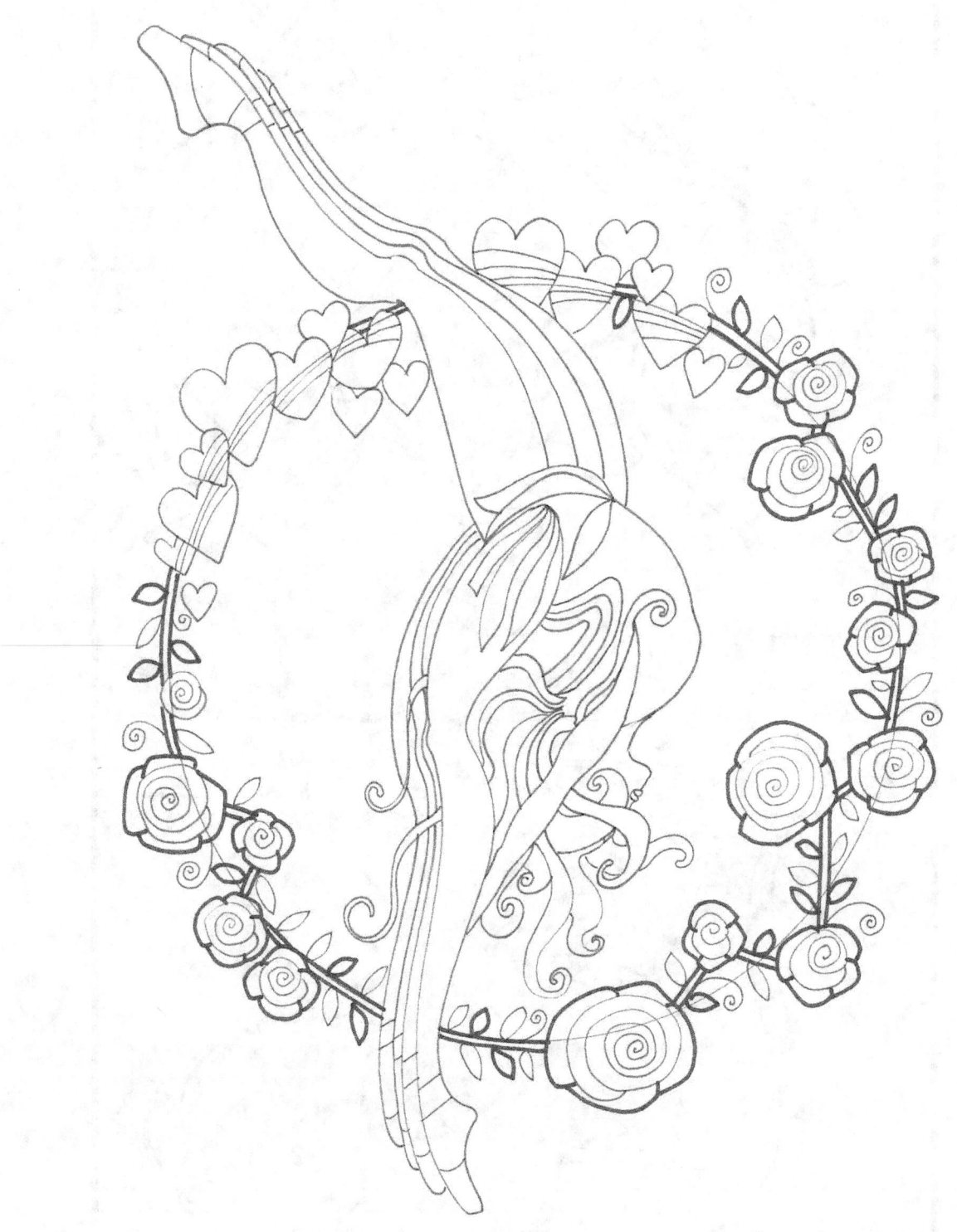

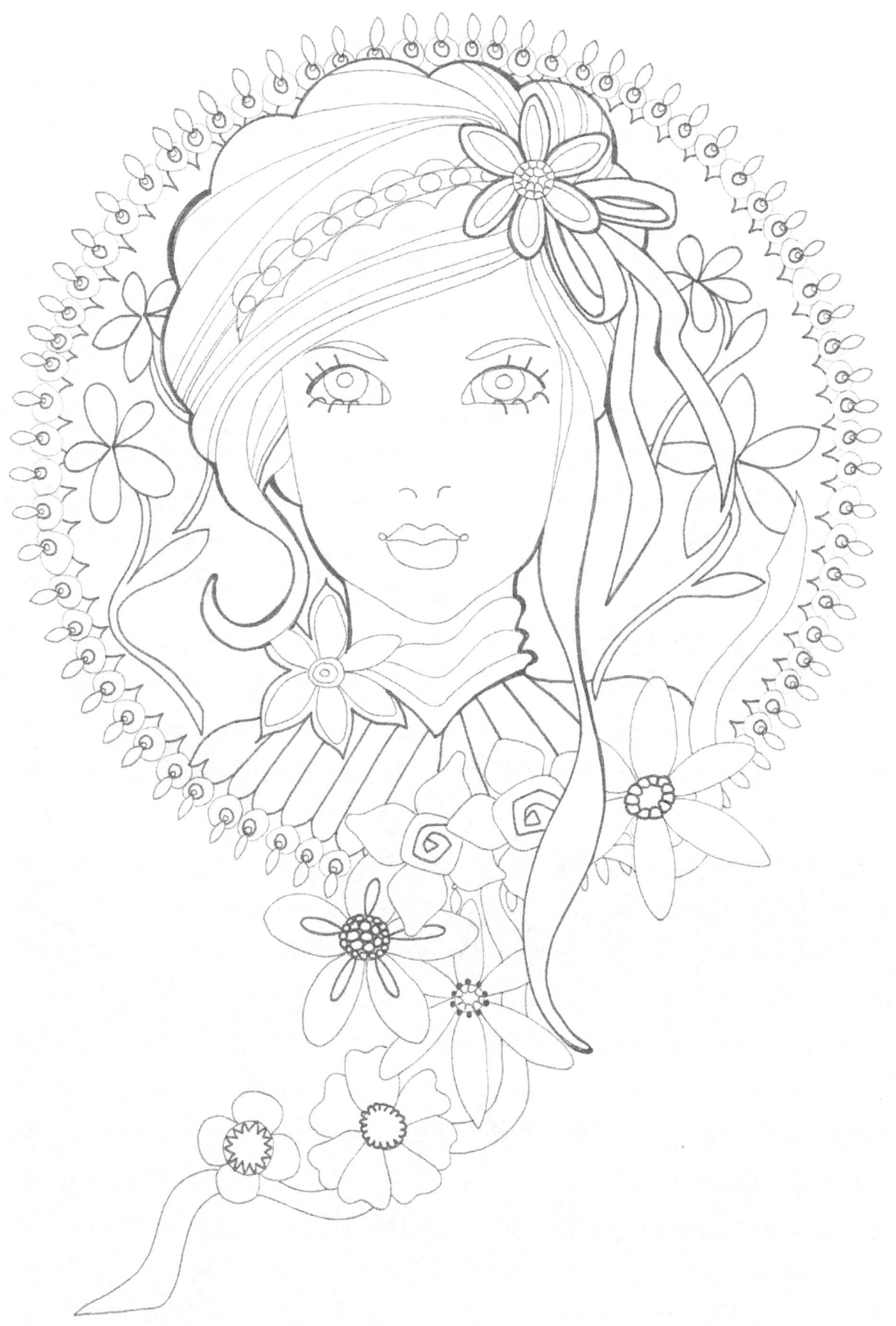

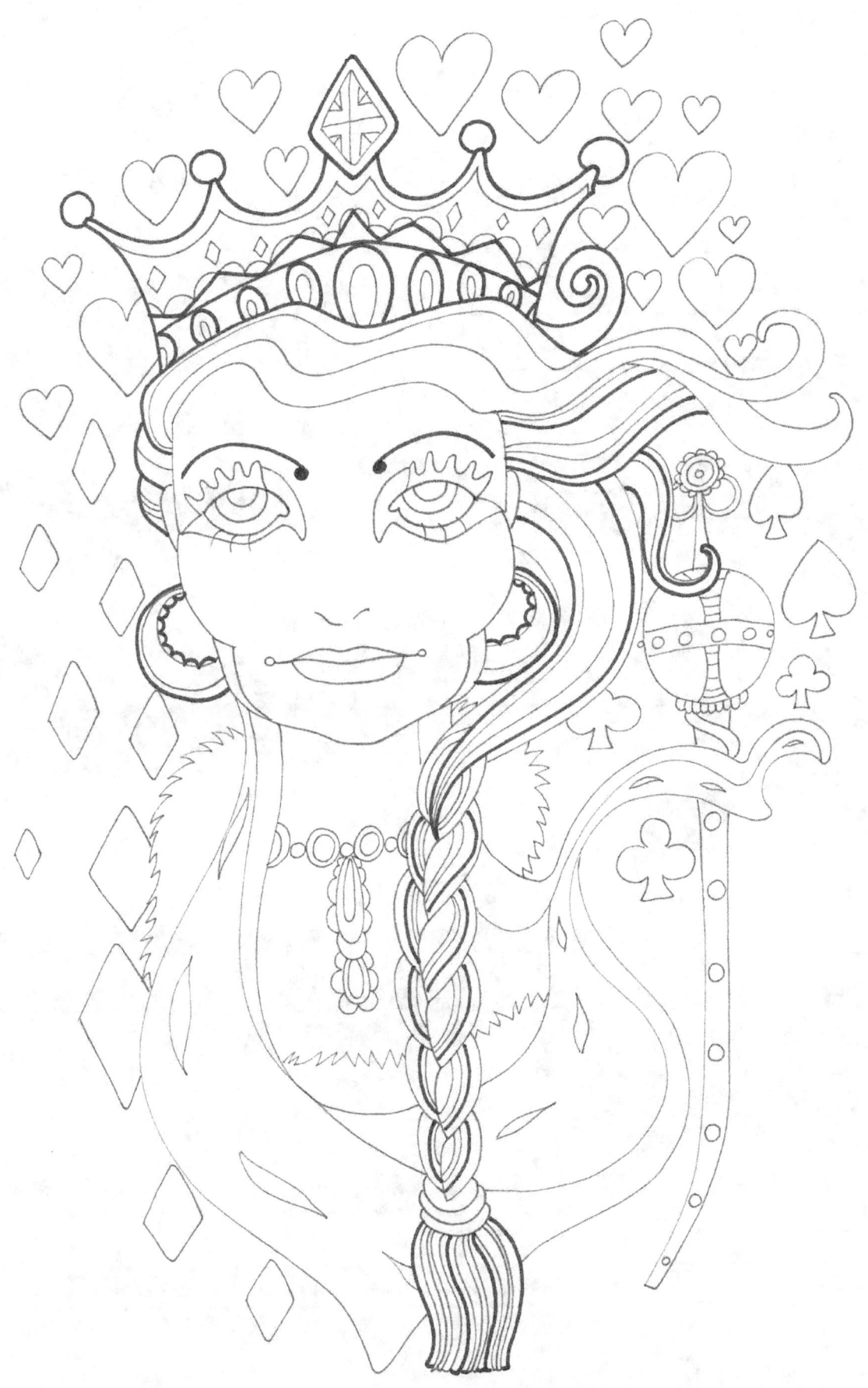

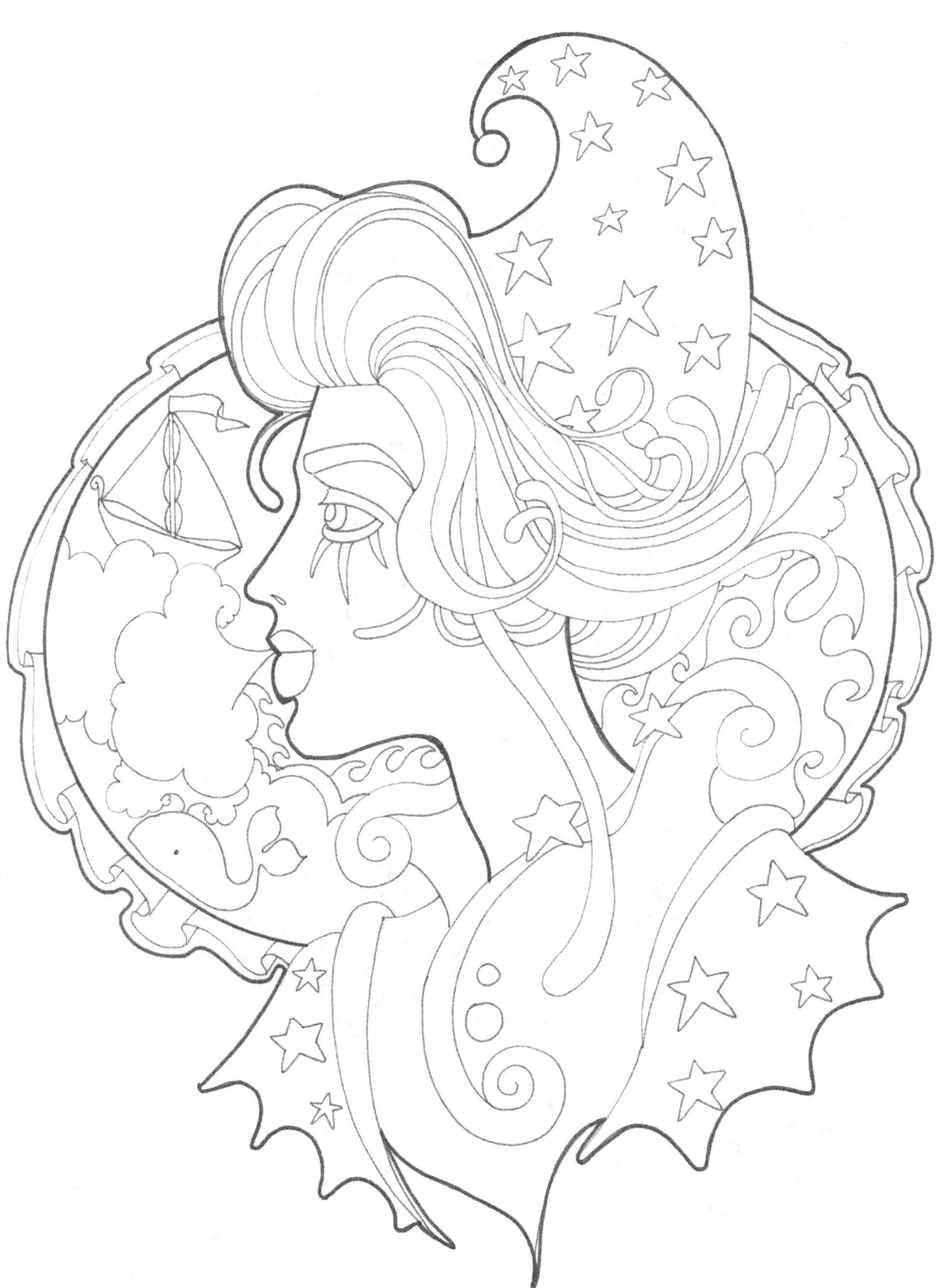

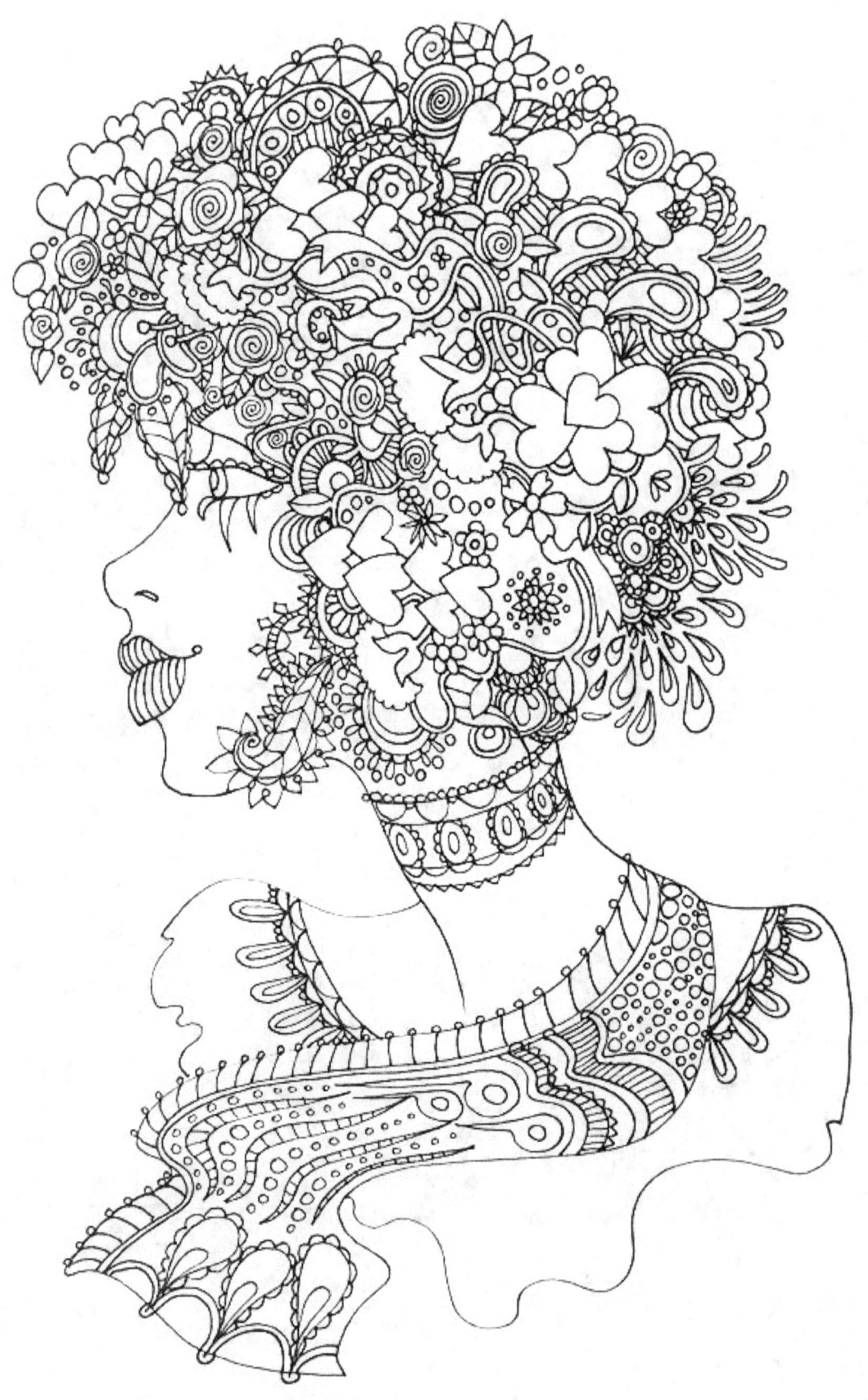

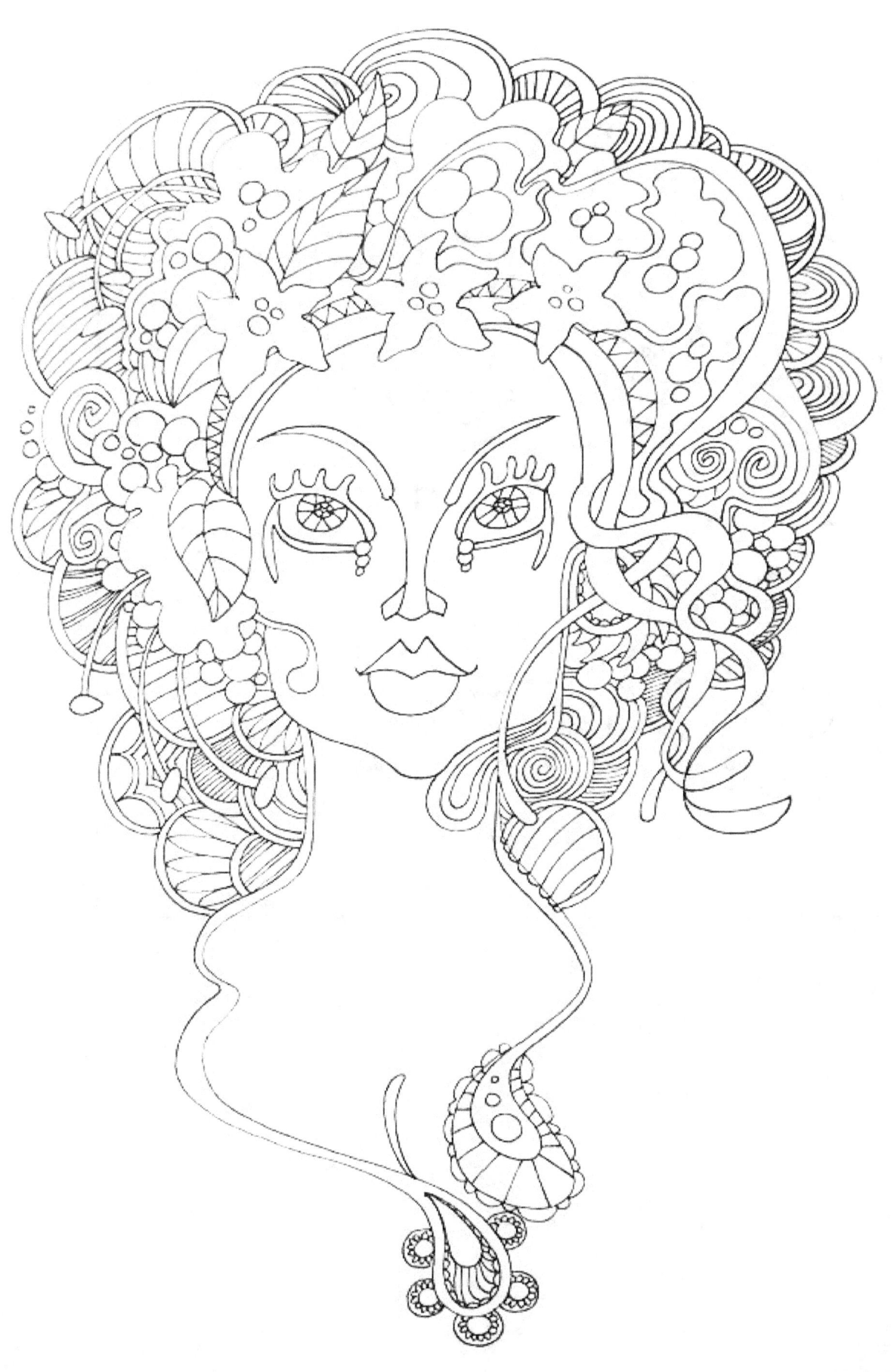

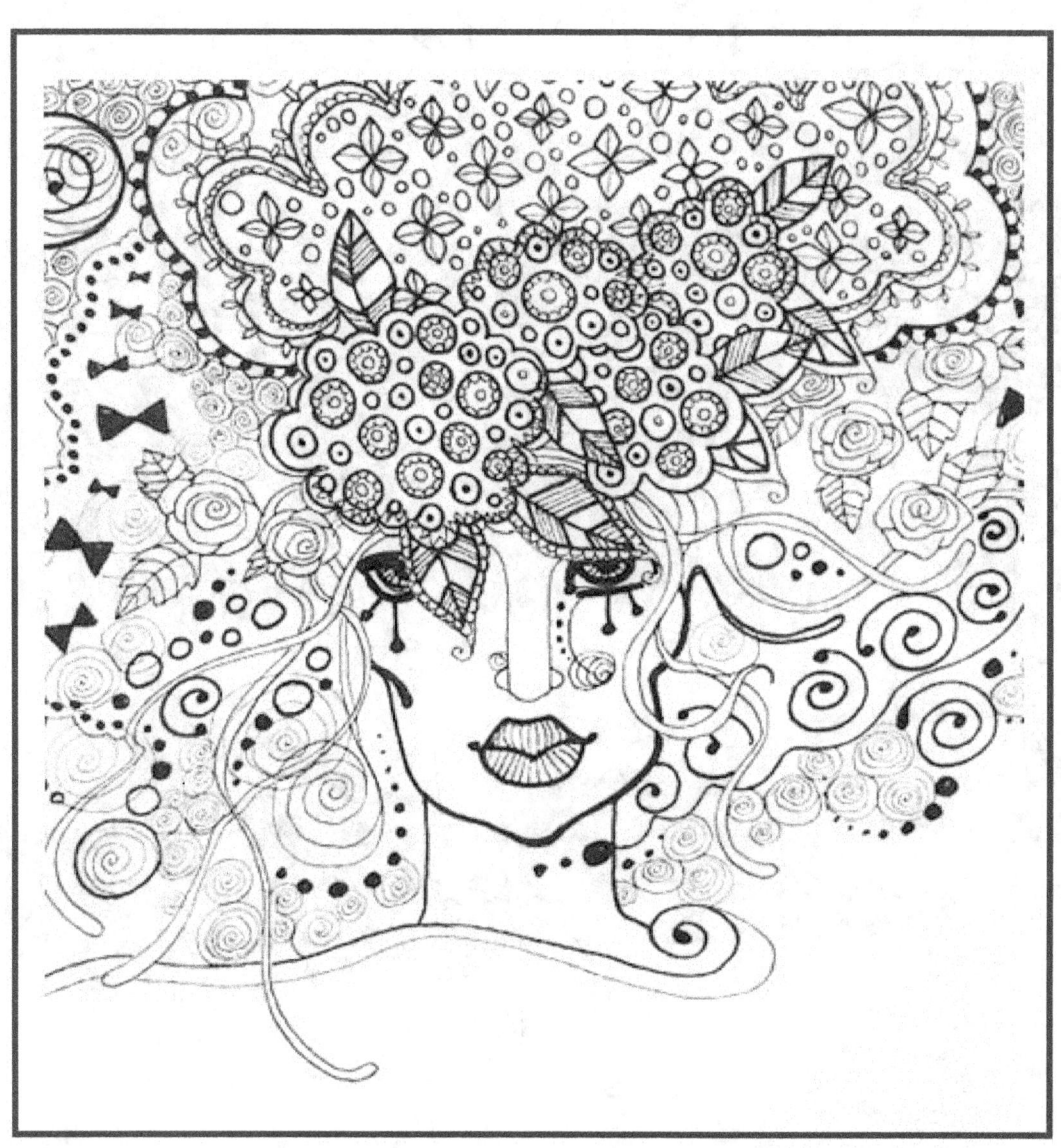